"What a breath of fresh air to all who share the journey of a child with special needs! Janet and Susan fully understand the heart of a parent who has received the life changing news and point the reader toward the greatest source of strength, the Lord Almighty."
—Renée Bondi
Speaker, Recording Artist, Author

"*A Special Kind of Love* is filled with special stories that will touch your heart and move you into action—when it comes to children with special needs, you can't help but sense God's pleasure and power on each and every child! Thank you, Susan and Janet, for the reminder!"
—Joni Eareckson Tada
President, Joni and Friends

"Parents of disabled children are often forgotten. Where do they find the support and encouragement they need? In this insightful and practical book. The stories of loss, struggles, and hope will benefit all parents of children with special needs."
—H. Norman Wright
Author and Speaker

A SPECIAL
KIND *of* LOVE

A SPECIAL KIND *of* LOVE

For Those Who Love Children with Special Needs

SUSAN TITUS OSBORN

JANET LYNN MITCHELL

Nashville, Tennessee

0-8054-2727-9

Published by Broadman & Holman Publishers,
Nashville, Tennessee

Dewey Decimal Number:
Subject Heading:

All Scripture verses are taken from the Holman Christian
Standard Bible® unless otherwise noted. Copyright © 1999, 2000,
2001, 2002, 2003 by Holman Bible Publishers. Also used is NIV,
New International Version, Copyright © 1973, 1975, 1984,
by International Bible Society.

Some of the names in the stories have been changed at the
contributors' requests.

1 2 3 4 5 6 7 8 9 10 09 08 07 06 05 04

DEDICATION

This book is dedicated to all the parents and caregivers of children with special needs. May God richly bless your families and your ministries.

IN LOVING MEMORY

Robbie Kosman, Eric Winter, James Haggerty, Jonathan Pulone, Timmy Anderson, Freddie Littauer, and Larry Littauer.

ACKNOWLEDGMENTS

We would like to thank all of those who contributed their stories and insights to this project. We'd especially like to thank Jeanne Pallos, Bonnie Hanson, Karen Kosman, Joyce Piper, Carolyn Hutchinson, Linda Evans Shepherd, Charlene A. Derby, and Jim Pierson for their contributions to this book.

Janet would also like to thank her husband, Marty, for making the journey of parenting their children one full of excitement, stability, and love. She would also like to thank her parents, George and Mary Lou Hepp, and her in-laws, Max and Agnes Mitchell, for their constant support in raising her children and encouragement in writing this book.

Susan would like to thank her husband, Dick, for his support and encouragement and her wonderful blended family of five kids who have provided her with ten wonderful grandchildren.

TABLE OF CONTENTS

FOREWORD

Every year—perhaps just to shock perspective parents—our government calculates the financial costs of "raising" a child. In 2002, for example, for a middle-income family the estimated costs incurred in raising a child from birth to age 18 rose to $160,140. That may be the average dollar cost of raising the average child, but as anyone who's been a parent knows, it's not just the financial costs that hit home as a parent. It's the emotional and spiritual price of raising a child that often cost us the most.

I think that's why I like Susan Titus Osborn and Janet Lynn Mitchell's book so much. It speaks to our hearts about the real costs, challenges, and rewards of raising a child with special needs. Parents who may feel empty and close to emotional bankruptcy will find huge deposits of hope and encouragement here. From the authors' biblical and practical insights to the wonderful real-life voices from dozens of parents of children with special needs, this book will make deposits in all these "special" parents' lives in ways that will help them in their health, heart, home, and faith.

Perhaps what my wife and I like best about this book is that it gave us what most of us need when we're dropped into an unfamiliar or even overwhelming situation. We don't just want an impersonal map handed to us when we're in an unfamiliar setting. We want a guide to take us by the hand, show us the landmarks, keep us out of places we shouldn't go, and take us to a positive destination and a place of rest. That's what you'll love about this book and the two "guides" who share so personally, honestly, and helpfully about the special kind of love God has for you—a love you will receive through loving your child.

—John Trent, Ph.D.
www.StrongFamilies.com

INTRODUCTION

If you've picked up this book, more than likely you love a child who has special needs. The awesome reality is that long before this child was born, God chose you to be a part of this child's life. Yes, God chose you with your talents, abilities, temperament, and inadequacies—knowing that you were perfect for the job.

At times we're sure you feel overwhelmed by the task before you and the questions that go unanswered. How does a mom respond to her three-year-old blind son when he asks, "But Mom, what does the color red look like?" What does a grandmother say to her ten-year-old granddaughter when she doesn't get asked to a slumber party because of the fear and added responsibility of inviting a child with juvenile diabetes? How does a teacher feel when she overhears a conversation indicating that her student was not picked for the team due to his unpredictable asthma? How does a father respond to his wheelchair-bound daughter who nightly waits by the phone anticipating an invitation to the winter formal—an invitation that never comes? How do you handle the day-by-day struggles, watching your child with special needs as he or she tries to fit into a typical world?

Parenting is challenging for most people. However, dealing with a handicapping condition, a chronic illness, or an emotional or social disability in a child presents an uphill challenge every day. Recent statistics show that more than 20 million families in the United States have a child with special needs—that's nearly one in three families.

For parents of these "special" kids, their worries go beyond grades, braces, and sports. Their worries begin at daybreak when they wonder if their child will be able to attend school that day. From praying that their child will not be made fun of, to praying for the strength their child will need to live his or her life fully and not give up, the parents' daily prayers have just begun.

After an exhausting day of answering their child's questions concerning the disability, managing medications, preparing proper foods, and making it to all doctor appointments, these parents truly need the comfort of sitting down, putting their feet up, and reading *A Special Kind of Love: For Those Who Love Children with Special Needs*.

This book is written for moms, dads, grandparents, foster parents, and extended families who live with "special" children on a day-by-day basis. The book is also designed for teachers, doctors, social workers, friends of the family, and pastors who work with these children. Through this book, families of children with special needs will meet other families who have been there, identify with their struggles, and read of their victories along the way.

In 1990 Janet Mitchell gave birth to a premature baby boy. Six weeks later her six-year-old daughter was admitted to the hospital, diagnosed with juvenile diabetes. Janet's two children were discharged the same day—one hooked up to a heart monitor and the other carrying a bag of tricks, insulin shots included. Awaiting her at home was an active four-year-old son.

Janet says, "When I was faced with my children's special needs, I felt paralyzed with fear. The calm, spur-of-the-moment lifestyle that my husband, Marty, and I had grown to appreciate was gone. The list of what I could do to fix the situation was short. I could not heal my children. I could not take away their pain or spare them the struggles of being different. I could not pretend that their problems did not exist.

"I did, however, find that I had some choices that only I could make. I had the choice of deciding what type of mother my children were to have. I could choose what type of home my children would experience and what people would influence their lives. And I discovered that I had the awesome privilege of teaching my children how to live."

In 1992 Susan married Dick Osborn. During their courtship, Dick's twenty-six-year-old mentally challenged son called Susan and said, "When you marry my dad, will you be my mom?" Susan immediately answered, "Yes!" Then Rick asked, "Won't you be my mom now? I don't want to have to wait until next August."

Susan has emotionally supported Rick through his marriage to Christina, who is also mentally challenged. Susan and Dick have mentored them both through the births of their two sons, Steven and Daniel, and the resulting overwhelming circumstances.

Susan says, "I love being Rick's mom! Even though Rick is now an adult who has chosen to live on his own, I accept phone calls from him on my toll-free number anytime day or night. I continually make time to listen to his latest concern or share in his joy. I realize that all his life Rick will mentally be a child, so he will always need me."

Susan is the grandmother of ten grandchildren. She has a thirteen-year-old granddaughter who is conquering a reading disability and an eleven-year-old granddaughter who has overcome a speech impediment. She is also grandma to Rick's two-year-old son, who is not yet talking and is showing signs of having special needs. Susan shares a close relationship with her cousin, Michelle, who in spite of her hearing impairment has become a cheerleader and has graduated from college. Through love and hard work by Susan's entire family, these handicapping conditions are being compensated for.

With a child who has special needs, we face challenges every day. Yet we can lean on God for our strength and anchor ourselves to him through his Word and prayer. He promises to sustain us. He also provides us with people whom he brings into our lives—friends, family members, and professionals. These "angels with skin on" will help and encourage us—whatever our situation—as we love and care for our children with special needs.

It is our prayer that through reading this book, your heart will be lifted and your journey made lighter since you will know *you are not alone*. May God sustain you and bless you.

Yours in him,
Susan Titus Osborn and Janet Lynn Mitchell

When I met Christ at the crossroads of life, He showed me which way to go by walking it with me.

—AUTHOR UNKNOWN

Chapter 1

WALKING IN FAITH

The Blow

CHARLOTTE ADELSPERGER

Jesus, please come. Whoever you are, wherever you are, please come! I don't know what else to pray. All I know is that the doctor has given us a blow. We have a seriously ill child.

I'm not ready, Lord. I'm still in shock. I can barely breathe. I can't believe this is happening to our family. I shuddered after I kissed my daughter on her forehead, then watched her being wheeled into an operating room. I didn't want to let her go, but in simple trust I committed her to you.

The agony of seeing my own child racked by pain is unbearable! Just earlier today I ran for a nurse, only to find out it was too soon for another pain shot. All I could do was wrap my arms around my little girl.

"Oh, Mommy, keep holding me," my little girl cried.

God, you know it's with a lump in my throat that I wrap my arms tightly around her. Silently, I wonder, *Who is going to hold me through this medical crisis?*

Just take me as I am, Lord, in all my confusion, in all my anger. Yes, anger. I'm angry at you for letting this happen to us. And I want to fight back at something. I want to fight for the well-being of our child! I would do anything to win health for this precious one I love so much.

I stop in this moment of stillness, and I know deep inside that the battle is not mine to win. It's beyond me. It's very complicated. And most of all, I realize that you did not send this trouble. It is part of the evil in our imperfect world. Oh, dear Lord, sustain my energies as a parent and don't let me crumble.

Please bless our child with your great love. Wrap us all in your everlasting arms right now and uphold us in the days ahead.

Many of you reading this book have found Charlotte Adelsperger's prayer an echo of your own words. "Jesus please come. . . . The doctor has given us a blow." Your child has been diagnosed with a medical problem and/or a special need. Others of you have picked up this book hoping to gain practical ways to encourage these parents in special families. Regardless—all of us love children with special needs!

We are on a journey, one we probably hadn't planned on taking. This trip may lead us across deserts, through valleys, and up mountains when our itinerary was set for Orlando. For some of us, this journey of loving and caring for a child with special needs began years ago. Yet for many of us, this journey has just begun.

Joshua 1:5 brings us encouraging words: "As I was with Moses, so I will be with you; I will never leave you nor forsake you" (NIV). Just as God was with Moses and Joshua, he has promised to be with us as we face our situations and our children's ongoing needs. Not only will God be with us, walking by our side, but we can count on him to lead us as we make this journey.

Isaiah 42:16 states: "I will lead the blind by ways they have not known, along unfamiliar paths I will guide them; I will turn the darkness into light before them and make the rough places smooth. These are the things I will do; I will not forsake them" (NIV).

Each day caring for our "special" children is a step of faith. We are on a journey, watching to see how God will meet our every need. We are on a journey where God will prove his faithfulness to us over and over again.

Janet's son, Joel, was born premature. Joel spent the first days of his life on life support as his family watched and waited. The days turned into weeks as Joel struggled with complications of an early birth. Six weeks went by. Joel gained strength. Janet and her husband, Marty, were in the process of learning how to care for Joel's special needs when their six-year-old daughter, Jenna, was suddenly hospitalized, diagnosed with juvenile diabetes.

The next two weeks seemed like a nightmare. Jenna and Joel remained in the hospital. Janet spread herself thin, spending time with each of her three children, including Jason, Marty and Janet's four-year-old typical son. Marty faced unbelievable challenges juggling the concerns of home life and his new job!

Tired and overwhelmed, Marty and Janet found themselves on a journey down a path they had never planned to travel, into a valley that had depths unknown. It was then that they began a day-by-day walk of faith, watching God meet their every need. They truly discovered that in spite of their circumstances, they did have "A Reason to Celebrate."

A Reason to Celebrate

JANET LYNN MITCHELL

Numbly, I left my husband, Marty, at the hospital where I had been visiting two of our children and headed for the grocery store. Since it was 11 p.m., I drove to the only store I knew was open twenty-four hours a day. I turned my car motor off and rested my head against the seat.

What a day, I thought to myself. With two of my young children in the hospital and a third waiting at Grandma's, I was truly spread thin. Today I had actually passed the infant CPR exam required before I could take eight-week-old Joel home from the hospital. *Would I remember how to perform CPR in a moment of crisis?* A cold chill ran down my spine as I debated my answer.

At the same time, I'd been learning the facts about juvenile diabetes and trying to accept my six-year-old daughter's diagnosis. In addition to the CPR exam, I'd spent the day reviewing how to test Jenna's blood and give her insulin shots. Exhausted, I reached for my grocery list that resembled more of a scientific equation than the food for the week. Now it was time to buy the needed food to balance the insulin that would sustain Jenna's life.

"Let's go, Janet," I mumbled to myself while sliding out of the car. "Tomorrow is the big day! Both kids are coming home from the hospital." It didn't take long before my mumbling turned into a prayer.

"God, I am soooo scared! *What-if* I make a mistake and give Jenna too much insulin, or *what-if* I measure her food wrong, or *what-if* she does the unmentionable—and sneaks a treat? And, God, what about Joel's apnea monitor? *what-if* it goes off? *What-if* he turns blue and I panic? The consequences are certain to be great!"

With a shiver, my own thoughts startled me. Quickly I tried to redirect my mind away from the *what-ifs*. I gave myself an emergency pep talk and recited what I knew to be true: "I can do all things through Christ who strengthens me. I can do all things . . ."

Like a child doing an errand she wasn't up for, I grabbed my purse, locked the car, and entered the store. The layout of the store was different from what I was used to. Uncertain where to find what I needed, I decided to walk up and down each aisle.

Soon I was holding a box of cereal, reading the label, trying to figure out the carbohydrate count and sugar content. *Would three-fourths of a cup of cereal fill Jenna up?* Not finding any sugar-free cereal, I grabbed a box of Kellogg's Corn Flakes and continued shopping. Pausing, I turned back. *Do I still buy Fruit Loops for Jason?* I hadn't even thought how Jenna's diagnosis might affect Jason, my typical four-year-old. *Is it OK if he has a box of Fruit Loops while Jenna eats Kellogg's Corn Flakes?*

Eventually I walked down the canned fruit and juice aisle. Yes, I need apple juice, but how much? Just how often will Jenna's blood sugar go low so she will need this lifesaving can of juice? Will a six-year-old actually know when her blood sugar is dropping? what-if. . . ? I began to ask myself again.

I held the can of apple juice and began to read the label. Jenna will need fifteen carbohydrates of juice when her sugar drops. But this can has thirty-two. Immediately I could see my hand begin to tremble. I tried to steady the can and reread the label when I felt tears leave my eyes and make their way down the sides of my face. Not knowing what to do, I grabbed a couple six-packs of apple juice and placed them in my cart. Frustrated by feelings of total inadequacy, I crumpled up my grocery list, covered my face in my hands, and cried.

"Honey, are you all right?" I heard a gentle voice ask. I had been so engrossed in my own thoughts that I hadn't noticed the woman who was shopping alongside me. Suddenly I felt her hand as she reached toward me and rested it upon my shoulder. "Are you all right? Honey, are you a little short of cash? Why don't you just let me . . ."

I slowly dropped my hands from my face and looked into the eyes of the silver-haired woman who waited for my answer. "Oh, no, thank you, ma'am," I said while wiping my tears, trying to gather my composure. "I have enough money."

"Well, honey, what *is* it then?" she persisted.

"It's just that I'm kind of overwhelmed. I'm here shopping for groceries so that I can bring my children home from the hospital tomorrow."

"Home from the hospital! What a celebration that shall be. Why, you should have a party!"

Within minutes this stranger had befriended me. She took my crumpled grocery list, smoothed it out, and became my personal shopper. She stayed by my side until each item on my list was checked off. She even walked me to my car, helping me as I placed the groceries in my trunk. Then with a hug and a smile, she sent me on my way.

It was shortly after midnight, while lugging the groceries into my house, that I realized the lesson this woman had taught me. "My kids are coming home from the hospital!" I giggled with joy. "Joel is off life support and functioning on a monitor. Jenna and I can learn how to manage her diabetes and give her shots properly. And just as God met my needs in a grocery store, he will meet each and every need we have. What a reason to celebrate!" I shouted to my empty house.

"Why, you should have a party," the woman had exclaimed.

And a party there would be!

The Mitchells did have a party the evening their children came home from the hospital. In fact, they celebrated often that next year as countless times Joel and Jenna returned to the hospital for care, always coming home to party hats.

"There were times my list of trials ran longer than my grocery list," said Janet. "I had to resist the temptation of looking at my circumstances and look instead to the One who was in control of them. I reminded myself often that I did have 'A Reason to Celebrate'!"

Like Janet and Marty, many of you might think your circumstances are overwhelming and beyond your control. You may feel that you are now in unfamiliar territory and the medical team surrounding your child is speaking Greek. You may wonder how your income will ever meet the requirements of your child with special needs and your family. And you may carry a burden, worrying about the future and how your child will manage. Rest assured that God hears your cries—from the cries of desperation to the silent tears you shed. He is listening, and he will meet your every need. You, too, have a reason to celebrate!

Martha Bolton has experienced God's faithfulness. Like many of us, God asked her to walk her journey of faith one day at a time, not knowing what tomorrow may bring. Even when all was dark and the light couldn't be seen, Martha offered "A Signature of Faith."

A Signature of Faith
MARTHA BOLTON

My husband and I stared at the hospital forms the nurse just handed me. "You need to read these and sign them," she stated matter-of-factly. A cold chill ran through my body as we began to read the consent-for-surgery forms. We could hardly believe that our precious two-year-old son, Tony, needed open-heart surgery. As is the case with surgical consent forms, it listed everything that could possibly go wrong during the operation. None of it was very comforting.

Tony had been dubbed a miracle baby by all who knew him. His gestation and birth hadn't been easy. With my past medical history that included a miscarriage at three months and a stillbirth at term, my pregnancy with Tony was deemed high risk. Throughout the nine months I saw my doctor almost every week and sometimes several times a week.

Yet once Tony was born and I held my precious son in my arms, I knew all the extra care and effort had been worthwhile. Unfortunately, Tony's newborn examination revealed congenital heart disease that someday might require surgery. My husband and I took a certain degree of solace in the vagueness of the word *someday*. But now *someday* was here, and the nurse was waiting for my signature. Three heart cauterizations had confirmed that Tony had a valve problem and a hole in his heart.

The nurse left us alone to read through the consent forms. We read and reread them as my palms began to sweat. I felt anxious about the operation. I could barely concentrate. All the "what-ifs" flooded my mind. I tried not to think about them, but I couldn't help myself. *What-if the surgery isn't successful? What-if something goes terribly wrong? What-if . . .* I couldn't bear to lose another baby.

Life had been so challenging, and finally things seemed to be going "right." God had given us the desires of our hearts. We had adopted two baby boys, Rusty and Matt, and now we were blessed with a third!

Finally we signed the forms, and then we prayed, trusting God to take care of our son through the surgery. We had been informed about the procedure and understood the seriousness of the operation. We had even been told, "If Tony has the slightest elevation in body temperature, his surgery will be canceled."

The following morning a nurse entered Tony's room. It was while taking his vital signs that she noticed Tony's fever. In minutes Tony's surgery was canceled, and we were on our way home.

Time after time we went through the same admittance routine only to be sent home the morning of surgery due to a spike in Tony's temperature. After several weeks of being on this emotional roller coaster, I cried out to God, "Please help us get on the other side of this crisis. I want you to take care of him through the surgery, but please, can't we get this behind us?"

That next week we drove Tony to the hospital again. Tony had a temperature, and his surgery was canceled. At this point I felt devastated. It didn't seem as if God was answering our prayers. I began to question him. "Why is Tony's surgery always delayed? Didn't you hear me, God?" I asked. "I want to get this over!"

Although God didn't answer me audibly, I did receive an answer. The following week I was flipping channels on the television set. On one station I noticed a news reporter standing in front of the hospital where Tony's surgery was to take place. Next to him stood a doctor. Evidently one of the staff physicians had been diagnosed with hepatitis.

Clearing his throat, the doctor stood in front of a microphone and began to speak: "At this time we are requesting that all children who have been examined by a staff physician in our pediatrics unit please return immediately for testing."

Without us realizing it, God had protected our son from exposure to hepatitis. Due to Tony's repeated fevers each time he had been admitted for surgery, he had been sent home from the hospital before a staff doctor ever examined him. Despite my desperate attempt to get God to hurry and do things my way, God knew we needed to wait.

Through this experience I learned that God's timing is perfect. Eventually Tony had his heart surgery and then a subsequent surgery. Both surgeries were successful, and Tony's prognosis is terrific.

Recently I was asked, if I had my life to live over again, would I want to do it without the pain? Without the hurt? Without those moments of crisis where all I could do was write my signature and trust God?

I thought for a moment and then knew my answer. "Naturally, I'd do anything to spare my child pain, but *my* pain? Probably not. Because walking by faith through the difficult places of life is where I've experienced God's faithfulness in a way I never knew before. Those places have changed my way of thinking, my values, and my priorities. They've also helped me to recognize and appreciate God's perfect timing.

In our journey of loving children with special needs, many of us have found times when we don't understand God's timing or the reason our whys are not answered. Martha found that God was not slow in acting on her behalf and that delays were his way of protecting her son. God is in control of our situations despite what we see, think, or feel. His timing is perfect!

Linda Evans Shepherd says, "When your handicapped child first enters your life, you are blinded by pain. But your sight returns as you see how precious is the gift God has given you." This was Charlene's experience when her son was diagnosed with a special need. Although Charlene did not yet fully understand, God knew "The Plan."

The Plan

CHARLENE A. DERBY

We had a plan for you before you were born.
You'd be the best that each of us had to offer—
Dad's teeth and Mom's toes,
Dad's grades and Mom's grace.
You were our little package of possibilities.

We watched you grow into a boy who liked construction,
Who had a bent for figuring things out.
Your favorite video was *Hard Hat Harry,*
And your favorite activity was building things,
Out of anything,
From sofa cushions to the dinner entrée.

We weren't prepared for the June morning
That shook the foundations of who we thought you
        were.
The report and the professionals who delivered it
Brought our perceptions tumbling down around us.

What did it all mean?
What was it you couldn't do, you
Whom we thought could do anything?

When the dust cleared,
We began to sift through the rubble,
Finding the bits we could keep and discarding the rest.
What remained was a boy who liked construction,
Who had a bent for figuring things out,
Whose favorite TV show was *Nova,*
Whose favorite activity was building things,
Out of anything,
From *Mad Science* projects to the sand at the beach.

Slowly, carefully, we began to rebuild
Selecting this, rejecting that,

Using new materials to build the scaffolding that would
    support you
While you reached for the sky.

God had a plan for you before you were born.
You'd be the best that he had to offer.

When the dust cleared, Charlene was able to see what she had lost sight
of. She now realized her son's abilities, not just his disabilities. She let
go of her dream of what she thought her son would be like and opened
her heart to who he was.

As with all children, those with special needs should be encouraged
by parents, teachers, and pastors to become as independent as possible.
They may struggle more and even take a different route to maturing, but
despite doubts and fears, many children with special needs grow up to
be productive, independent, well-balanced individuals who enjoy life.

"It was my attitude that needed an adjustment," said one parent.
"I knew that as the parent it was my responsibility to set the emotional
tone and acceptance in my home. I had to erase my archaic ideas and
concepts concerning handicapped children and educate myself. I also
had to ask God to help me see my situation through his eyes."

How we respond to our children's medical crises and their never-
ending needs leaves a lasting picture for them—ultimately showing
them what we truly believe. Cassie's father, too, knew that his daughter
was learning lessons from the example he set. He tells his story in
"When I Grow Up."

When I Grow Up
CASSIE'S FATHER

"Dad, I don't have a dream," my twelve-year-old daughter announced
as she entered the kitchen. Sounding serious, she continued, "I don't
know what to be or what I could even attempt to become!"

"What? When? Slow down, Cassie," I said, trying to figure out what
she was talking about.

"When? When I grow up!" she clarified.

Now I understood. My daughter had begun to contemplate her future, and in the process she was seeing only the obstacles. Her physical limitations were limitations, and her possibilities were simply impossibilities.

Before I could get a word in, Cassie explained, "Today at school our assignment was to stand up in front of the class and share what we want to be when we grow up. I have no idea, so I prayed extra hard that the recess bell would ring just to give me extra time to think! And it did!"

"Well, Cassie, tell me what happened?"

"I went out to recess and sat on the bench. Then an idea came to me, and I went to find Mrs. Riley. I told her about my problem and asked, 'Do you think that instead of sharing what I want to be, I could share with the class what type of person I want to become?'"

Then listening carefully, I sat down at the kitchen table as my daughter repeated the speech she had given to her class.

"When I grow up," Cassie said with her eyes fixed on mine, "I want to be like my parents. You see, my mom is kind and patient. She laughs a lot and makes people feel special. My dad is a hard worker, but he always has time to spend with our whole family. My parents love each other and love me. They honor God and are good citizens. Yep, even though I've lost my legs, and I don't yet know what I'll be when I grow up, I know I can become a great person—just like my mom and just like my dad!"

It's true that many of our children with special needs can't envision their futures. Some may see their possibilities yet are unaware of the diverse career and job opportunities available. Understandably, many parents share their child's lack of vision and see their child's limitations—as true limitations.

"Dad, I don't have a dream," twelve-year-old Cassie said. "I don't know what to *be* or what I could even attempt to become!" The great news for Cassie and others is found in Jeremiah 29:11. "'For I know the plans I have for you,' declares the LORD, 'plans to prosper you and not to harm you, plans to give you hope and a future'" (NIV).

Cassie does have a future, one that is designed by the hand of her Almighty Creator. For today, it's OK that Cassie doesn't know what her future holds. It's enough just knowing *who* holds her future!

For Christians this journey of faith that God has asked those of us who love kids with special needs to walk is one of trusting him with our everyday concerns and with all the uncertainties tomorrow may bring. No, it's not easy, and often the challenges are far beyond what we feel we can manage. Yet God promises us that he will never leave us or forsake us. We will not walk this journey alone because God is and always will be by our side.

But how will we know if we are making the right decisions pertaining to our child's needs? What do we do when we just don't know what to do?

Scripture says that God is dependable and will direct us on our journey of caring for our children. Isaiah 30:21 says, "Whether you turn to the right or to the left, your ears will hear a voice behind you, saying, 'This is the way; walk in it'" (NIV).

After we have prayed and asked God for wisdom, we wait fully expecting him to answer. Yes, there are times when we weigh the positives and the negatives and then step out in faith. Just as we can depend on God to help us make the right decisions, we can depend upon him to stop us and prevent us from making the wrong ones. God is willing and able to assume full responsibility for a life wholly yielded to him. As we place our children in God's hands, he then is in charge of their care.

John Paul's mom learned what it was like to trust God with the circumstances concerning her son. She saw that God was faithful and he heard her prayers. Not only did Yadira realize that in her darkest moments God was there, but also John Paul was assured that God was taking care of him. With God doing the worrying, there's not much left to do except enjoy our kids!

In God's Hands

YADIRA PACO

My son, John Paul, has cerebral palsy. Recently I took him to a new neurologist, hoping to have an MRI taken to see if John Paul had made any neurological progress. Instead of ordering a new MRI, the doctor reviewed John Paul's first one that was taken when he was six months old. "But Doctor," I wanted to say, "John Paul is now six. Don't you think we need an updated test?"

After reviewing the original MRI, the doctor leaned against the wall and folded his arms. "There's no need for a new MRI," the doctor said with a sigh. Then he added, "You need to be realistic. John Paul's future is going to be very difficult. If your sights are set on college, you're aiming too high—forget it. You need to be satisfied that he is using a walker and verbalizing some words. Listen, no matter how hard you push him, it won't do any good. Somehow you need to resign yourself to the fact that this is the life your son will lead."

When I left the neurologist's office, I felt devastated. Driving home, I fought back tears. *Why did the doctor present such a bleak future for my son?* My thoughts traveled back to the time when John Paul had first been diagnosed. And now, years later, I repeated my cry, *Why did this happen to my son?*

For a moment I felt a tinge of the anger I had felt toward God when I first heard John Paul's diagnosis of cerebral palsy. At that time I became so angry with God that I stopped praying and refused to go to church. Yet it seemed that no matter how far I tried to get from God, he didn't leave me alone. For a year and a half I struggled, trying not to allow God to love me. Yet I found it impossible to run away from my Creator.

Once again I picked up my Bible. God's words in Deuteronomy 31:8 spoke to me: "The LORD himself goes before you and will be with you; he will never leave you nor forsake you. Do not be afraid; do not be discouraged" (NIV).

Then I realized that even during my darkest moments, God had been there for me all along. I made up my mind that I wasn't going to let a negative diagnosis from a doctor shake my faith.

That next week I went about my usual schedule and tried to look beyond the doctor's devastating news. I focused my thoughts on the positive and applied God's promises from his Word.

A month later John Paul's teacher called. "Mrs. Paco, I wanted you to know that John Paul is meeting all the goals we set for him. He's even interacting, playing with the other kids, and trying to talk to them."

I couldn't believe it. I was thrilled! This news reaffirmed to me that God was there for John Paul. I thanked him for teaching my son new things.

Today John Paul is walking without a walker, and he is talking more. He is a bright boy. My mother speaks to him in Spanish, and he understands both Spanish and English. Recently he has learned how to use the computer and the mouse.

Day-by-day I continue to see progress. God has shown his presence in John Paul's life in all these little ways. John Paul's teacher said that if he continues to improve, next year he will be put with kids with moderate problems rather than severe.

Recently I picked my son up at day care. As I opened the car door to help him in, John Paul looked at me and said, "Mommy, God is telling me that he is going to take care of me."

Hearing these words, I finally relaxed. I placed John Paul and his future in God's hands and decided to take one day at a time. I don't want to miss the little things along the way. I believe God wants me to just enjoy my son, and that's what I'm going to do!

*In the darkest day, we can still hope in the unsearchable riches
and the all-sufficient grace and the unconquerable power of God.*
—WILLIAM BARCLAY

Chapter 2
HAVING HOPE IN HOPELESS SITUATIONS

The Journey Starts
LINDA EVANS SHEPHERD

Covering my eyes with my hands, I tried to block the horror of the afternoon as I huddled under the emergency room window. A storm raged outside the hospital, while another storm raged within my heart. The more I fought, the more clearly I could see myself behind the wheel of my car.

The scene swirled through my thoughts: eighteen-month-old Laura snuggling in her car seat, the red taillights reflecting on the damp pavement, my foot reaching for the brakes, my car lurching across the dividing line, the accelerating minivan . . .

A thunderous explosion of metal ripping through metal roared in my ears as my body flopped like a limp rag doll against my seat belt. The silence that followed chilled my heart. Why . . . why wasn't my baby crying?

I turned to the backseat, still expecting to reassure eighteen-month-old Laura's frightened, blue-gray eyes. Instead I stared into a jagged, twisted metal hole.

Slipping out of my seat belt, I clawed my way through the wreckage. I was afraid of finding Laura's body shattered in the crumpled ruins. Instead I found her in the middle of the freeway, still fastened in her car seat, dazed and still.

A doctor rushed past me, bringing me back to the present as he slammed the heavy emergency room doors. I caught a glimpse of the staff's continued fight for Laura's life. "Jesus, help them!" I pleaded.

Soon I was ushered into the hospital waiting room, and shortly thereafter my husband, Paul, arrived, damp with rain and tears. I rushed into his arms.

"Is . . . is she going to be OK?" he asked.

"I don't know," I choked. "She has a fractured skull."

We sat together, silently, staring at the floor, our voices stolen by shock and grief.

The days that followed the car accident were critical as Laura fought for her life. Each time Laura thrashed with seizures, her nurses rushed her to X-ray. I stumbled behind, blinded by grief. Each CAT scan sent Laura back to surgery for the relief of the volcanic pressure building in her brain.

"We're sorry," the doctor finally said, "but Laura will never awaken. She's in a vegetative state."

As only a mother could know, I knew Laura was not a vegetable, but a little girl held captive by her body. Looking at my sleeping beauty, I constantly cried, *How much longer, God?*

Days turned into months. One evening a physician stood in the doorway of Laura's hospital room, listening to the mechanical breathing of Laura's respirator. He stared at the floor as his words chilled the air, "Linda, Laura is not going to recover. You might as well . . ."

His unspoken words screamed, "End it now! Pull the plug!"

Like a stalking hunter he awaited my response. I swallowed hard, knowing we were playing a dangerous game, a game Laura couldn't afford for me to lose. I wearily tried to hide in silence, waiting for the deadly moment to pass. Finally I found my voice. "But my daughter is not dead!" I announced, fighting to sound calm.

I struggled to avoid an emotional breakdown that would give the doctor control. I took a deep breath and clenched my fists. "Laura—Laura has too much brain activity! Besides, what makes you think she's not going to recover?"

The doctor pulled me into his office. "You need to face the facts. Half of Laura's brain has been destroyed."

Frowning, I answered, "But half of her brain is intact. Are you telling me you can scientifically factor the impact my love, faith, and prayers will have on this child's future?"

"No," the doctor grudgingly admitted.

I pressed, "Then your prognosis is only a guess. You see, God can take Laura if he wants her. He has my permission, but he doesn't need me to pull her plug!"

The doctor sighed. He rose, and I followed him out of his office. I leaned against Laura's doorjamb and closed my eyes, trying to still my rapid heartbeat. *This victory is won, but how many other battles are left to fight?* I wondered. I thought of Psalm 23:4: "Even though I walk through the valley of the shadow of death, I will fear no evil, for you are with me; your rod and your staff, they comfort me" (NIV).

Lord, I prayed, please see me through. For my hope and comfort are in you and you alone.

∞

God gave Linda the strength she needed to face her circumstances. He listened to her prayers and used Scripture to comfort her. In her book *Encouraging Hands, Encouraging Hearts*, she offers these words of encouragement:

> Our lives are made of changing seasons. Seasons of grief and suffering often seem overwhelming. With no hope for relief, the waiting can seem to last forever.
>
> When my dad was a boy, he planted a peanut patch. On the surface, it looked like nothing was happening, so he dug up his crop. Of course, the peanuts, developing all along, stopped developing after that. But Dad learned a valuable lesson that day: Growth and change are taking place even when we cannot see them.
>
> Sometimes we are in a season of waiting. We pray, hope, and suffer, but we can't see the results—because they are happening beneath the surface. Our inability to see, however, does not mean that God is not working.

∞

When we are having problems coping with suffering, we need to allow ourselves to grieve our losses. Jeanne Pallos shares a tool that helped her face the losses in her own life.

G—Give the loss a name. Identify the trauma or loss. Name the illness, the disability, the accident. Learn about it.

R—Reexperience the loss. The most important thing is to feel the pain involved with the loss. Talk about what happened, think about it, or write about it. Don't try to change your feelings.

I— Identity what you are feeling about the loss. There is no shortcut to healing. Admit what you are feeling. It's OK to say, "I'm so hurt," or "I'm so disappointed," or "I can't understand why this is happening."

E—Express your feelings to others. Find supportive people with whom you can share your experience and feelings. Join a support group, find someone you can call anytime, seek professional counseling, or find someone to pray with.

F—Find freedom by allowing yourself to grieve to completion. This final step may take a few hours, days, weeks, or years. Don't condemn yourself for what you are feeling or how long it takes to move to a place of acceptance. Give yourself permission to take as much time as you need to work through your loss.

Yes, grieving for our children is a normal and necessary step in our healing process. A number of experts have come up with various stages in the grief process. The following six stages best depict what we might experience.

- Shock—having our idealistic dreams crushed when we discover our child is unhealthy or handicapped.
- Denial—protecting ourselves from the shock, not believing this is happening, and making excuses for our child's behavior or symptoms.
- Anger—outrage because of the situation, which we then direct toward our child, our spouse, other family members, God, or anyone else we can find to lash out at.
- Guilt—wondering if we did something to cause our child's illness or condition, or if we didn't do something to prevent it.
- Depression—feeling emotionally paralyzed and isolated from friends and family members.
- Acceptance—turning to God and finding hope. Through his

strength we will face the future together and be able to deal with whatever happens.

Experts agree that parents and caregivers of children with special needs will experience these phases in varying degrees throughout the lives of their children. Yet we all need to remember that God cares for us and shares our pain. We also need to take to heart the words of Amber's daddy in the following story, "We Believe in Miracles."

We Believe in Miracles

AMBER'S DADDY

"Daddy, pray for me again," seven-year-old Amber pleaded. "Pray that God will fix my body and make it work right!"

I felt my heart skip a beat. My precious daughter was coming to me, her daddy, and asking me to help her. She was asking me to talk to God on her behalf, and she was depending on God to answer my prayer.

"Daddy, will I get the miracle tonight, or will it take a week or two? I think I really need it now."

Instantly, a lump formed in my throat, and I was at a loss for words. I thought about the countless nights I lay awake, asking God to do just that—heal my child. And now my child was expecting answers.

I leaned down, scooped up Amber, and held her in my arms. "Amber," I whispered in her ear, "Daddy prays for you every day and night." Choking on my tears, I continued, "Yes, baby, we're waiting for our miracle."

That night as I tucked Amber in bed, I realized my daughter was living out her Christian faith—just as I had taught her. I realized she believed that God loved her and would take care of her. Yet, at age seven, I wondered what her faith might do if God, for his reasons alone, chose not to heal her.

The following morning I poured Amber's favorite cereal into a bowl while Amber reached for the spoons. Somehow, someway, I needed to have a little chat with her about the miracle she was waiting for. I opened my mouth to speak, but Amber spoke first. "Daddy," she said, "I didn't get my miracle last night."

"No, Amber. I know you didn't."

"Well, that's OK because I've been thinking. You know my friend, Sandy? Well, her mom and dad don't believe in God and don't believe in miracles, so I'm really lucky! You see, Daddy, it's a miracle that we can ask for a miracle!"

Staring into my cereal, I listened to my daughter's words. She was not upset that she had not been healed. She was excited about the fact that we knew the greatest miracle of all. She knew we believed in the God of miracles!

"Yes, Amber, we do. We believe in miracles!"

Miracles do happen. God used the wisdom of doctors and the proper medications to bring about Amber's healing, as her cancer is now in remission. Yet for many of us, our children's special needs are not healed, and we are left to face each day, encouraging our children to make the best of things.

Sometimes our miracle is finding the right doctor at just the right time. Other times it's the fact that our child was spared the complications of having the flu. Some days our miracle might be simply having the strength and courage to face another day.

What do we do when the miracle we've hoped for never arrives? What do we do when our child's heart is breaking and ours is skipping a beat watching her suffer?

Scripture tells us that when all human reason for hope was gone, Abraham hoped. Because Abraham knew God and had faith, he did not give up. He knew God's promises and waited for them to be fulfilled.

We, like Abraham, believe that God can make the impossible possible. And when there is no miraculous cure, the Holy Spirit will comfort us, strengthen us, and help us cope with our day-to-day struggles. Janet shares such a miracle in "The Day My Daughter Lost All Hope."

The Day My Daughter Lost All Hope
JANET LYNN MITCHELL

"Don't you know my miracle will never come. There will never be a cure!" my daughter screamed from the backseat of the car.

I steadied my hands on the steering wheel as Jenna continued to rant and rave. I tried to swallow the unwelcome lump that immediately formed in my throat. Not finding a single word that could or would change the situation, I remained quiet as tears stung my eyes. "Lord, they're working on a cure. Please guide their progress. Lord, my daughter has lost all hope . . ."

"I'm tired of feeling sick. I'm tired of being tired. I'm sick and tired of being sick and tired! It's just too hard!" Jenna sobbed from behind me. "Mom, I just don't think I can do it anymore," she said as her voice faded.

Her words cut deep. I knew that without hope her heart would break. Wishing that this conversation were occurring anywhere but on the freeway, I fought traffic and slowly made my way to the off-ramp. Periodically I looked into my rearview mirror only to see Jenna's penetrating eyes gazing back at me. The unnerving silence was interrupted only with the sound of my blinker.

Jenna was right. I knew that it had been years since she truly felt good. I knew that she had shown great courage for the past twelve years and that it was tough fighting her disease. I, too, was tired of daily watching my daughter as she tended to her catheter, injected herself with the proper medications, and experienced the unpredictable side effects that came with her disease and treatment. I, too, wanted to scream, "I'm also sick and tired of you being sick and tired!"

I loved my daughter, and watching her in such emotional and physical pain made me ache all over! If there were only a way, I would take her illness upon myself; I'd give her my health and bear her infirmity. But I knew that this was not a possibility, and I felt helpless, not knowing how to console her.

Within minutes I pulled into the first parking lot I could find and parked the car. I stepped out and then crawled into the backseat where my teenage daughter lay motionless across the bench seat. I wrapped my arms around her and brushed her hair away from her eyes, hoping she would open them and look into mine. For moments I just sat and held her, praying that God would renew her strength and will to live.

What does a mother say to her child who is living a nightmare, praying that she'd someday soon wake up? What words, if any, could bring comfort? What do you do when your child loses all hope? Not knowing the answers, I spoke from my heart, hoping to reach Jenna's.

"Jenna, I need you to look at me. I need to know that you really understand what I am about to say."

She turned her head, which now lay in my lap, toward me. She opened her eyes and began to repeat her words of hopelessness. Gently I placed my finger against her lips.

"Honey, today you're tired, and you've lost all hope. Today you can rest in my arms and let me hope for you. You can be assured that my hope is endless and so is my love. I'm so proud of you."

Jenna interrupted me with a slight smile. "Mom, if you can hope, I guess I can too. And Mom, tell me again that your hope is forever."

"It's forever, baby. My hope is forever!"

Living with a chronic illness is difficult. Knowing that each day the person will face the side effects of his or her disease can be depressing. For a child the contrast of physically feeling bad and the desire of wanting to fit in can be overwhelming.

Hope is the ingredient that brings the excitement of tomorrow. It involves putting one's faith into action when doubting would be easier. It believes that God has made a promise to take care of us, and it anticipates this to happen. Hope is what Janet provided for Jenna the day Jenna felt like giving up.

Mikayla's parents also had hope. They prayed, risked being misunderstood, and obeyed Scripture. Mikayla definitely had "Two Persistent Parents."

Two Persistent Parents

SANDRA L. STEELE

Due to complications during delivery, our daughter, Mikayla, suffered the consequences of a paralyzed arm. My husband was unusually quiet, and my heart felt heavy as we drove home from the hospital. *Why had God allowed this to happen?*

As the days went by, I fought a mounting panic as I wondered how difficult life would be for my precious child. "Lord God, please help us. Show us what to do to help our child," my husband and I prayed. Yet our prayers seemed unanswered. We placed Mikayla's name on our church prayer line. It was our goal to bombard heaven's doors on Mikayla's behalf.

Every day brought new hurts. If Mikayla's condition were life threatening, would our church family show more concern? Don't they know I long for their encouragement and support? I'd seen parents show more concern over a child's skinned knee than our church showed over our child's handicap. I felt deserted by those I expected to rally by my side.

One Sunday morning I finally broke my silence and shared my concerns for my daughter. I was stunned at the responses I received. "You need to increase your faith, and then God will touch Mikayla's arm," one suggested.

"At least it's only her arm. It could have been much worse," another said while adding salt to my wounds.

"I'm sure this is part of God's plan," I was told. "You watch and see how God uses Mikayla's injury to bless others."

As fast as I could, I half nodded and turned my head. *Does she think that God caused Mikayla's difficult birth and injury so that others might be blessed? What will happen the next time God's people need a blessing? Will God take Mikayla's legs?* I thought sarcastically.

Could it be that these folks didn't know what to say, so they said what first came to their minds? Or did they really believe these statements of insensitivity and half-truths? Oh how I wished they had simply offered a hug and a silent prayer.

My husband and I clung to Scripture for comfort and guidance. James 5:14 stood out in our minds. We read it again and again: "Is anyone among you sick? He should call for the elders of the church, and they should pray over him after anointing him with olive oil in the name of the Lord."

"I get it, Sandra!" my husband shouted while pondering this passage again. "The verse says if anyone is sick he should call for the elders of the church. Don't you see? We've been waiting for the church to come to us, and James 5:14 says that we're the ones who need to do the calling!"

My husband and I acted on this verse and asked the elders of our church to lay hands on our four-month-old daughter and pray for her healing. They came and they prayed.

Four days later Mikayla showed signs of nerve regeneration. At six months she demonstrated signs of bicep movement. Then another miracle occurred, as she now has 50 percent usage of her arm—a direct result of two persistent parents and answered prayer.

Mikayla's parents met obstacles, piercing words from brothers and sisters in their church. Yet they were persistent in their faith. They prayed, hoped, and applied Scripture to their lives. When they read in Scripture that they should call upon the elders, they called them. Today, although they know what it is like to hurt for a child, they also know how it feels to experience answered prayer!

Sandra says, "When someone is hurting, you don't have to offer words. Provide a hug and a prayer." Many times we don't know what to say when our loved ones are experiencing a difficulty. Often we try to say something profound. Yet we don't think about the negative message we might be communicating. Our words should be like honeycomb—sweet, loving, and kind. Words such as "I'm so sorry this has happened," or "What can I do to help?" soothe those who are hurting.

Like Mikayla's parents, Marty and Janet experienced a time when all seemed dark. Janet shares her story in "The Blessing Jar."

The Blessings Jar

JANET LYNN MITCHELL

Life hadn't been easy the past year. In fact, the list of difficult circumstances ran longer than my grocery list. I felt exhausted. Yet my strength was needed to help hold the pieces together.

"Why do I have to take four shots a day?" Jenna Marie, my kindergartener, asked repeatedly. The explanation of being diagnosed with juvenile diabetes didn't seem to satisfy her.

"Just how big is the tank that Uncle Rusty is driving? How far away is the Gulf War? Who is this guy Saddam anyway?" my four-year-old son, Jason, questioned.

Beep, Beep, Beep . . . the steady rhythm of my premature baby Joel's heart monitor was heard in the background—our moment-by-moment reminder of how fragile life really is.

Marty, my husband, and I had learned to expect the unexpected. We were constantly anticipating the bad and bracing ourselves for it. Lately we had lost our focus. The challenges of life so overwhelmed us that we did not see the blessings God provided us daily.

As a family, we regularly read of God's faithfulness to Moses, Joseph, and David. "Why can't we read about God's faithfulness to us— the Mitchells?" our children asked.

At a loss for words, I looked to my husband, hoping he would answer.

After a long moment of silence, he said, "We can and we will! Jenna, go get Daddy's special note cards out of the middle desk drawer in the study. Jason, get the box of crayons and markers."

The children hurried off, full of excitement. Daddy had an idea, and they couldn't wait to hear it.

I sat pondering. I couldn't help but wonder what my nonseminarian husband might be thinking.

When the children returned, we all sat Indian-style on the family room floor. Everyone focused their eyes on Daddy as he began to speak. "There are times in our lives when we don't see God's blessings right away. Sometimes they are disguised, and the things we once thought of as bad or scary turn into wonderful blessings. Think of a caterpillar. He isn't very pretty. And I wonder if it is a little bit scary for him to seal off the cocoon he entwined around himself. I wonder if it is dark in there. I wonder if Mr. Caterpillar screams, 'Let me out of here! I can't breathe!' But then one day, just at the right time, we see something happen. We see God's plan, the miracle of a beautiful butterfly."

Reaching for the note cards that Jenna clutched tightly in her hands, Marty continued, "Let's think back and remember how God has taken care of us and blessed our family. Then we'll write these blessings on the special note cards."

"But Daddy, we can't write words," Jason said.

"We couldn't read them even if we wrote them!" Jenna chimed in.

"You're right," Daddy replied. "But you can draw!"

For the next half hour our family remembered, drew, laughed, and even shed a few tears as we recorded God's faithfulness to the Mitchells.

After tucking the children into bed and saying good night to Marty, I went out to the garage. I dug around a cluttered shelf and found an old dusty pickle jar. I dragged out an old set of "puffy paint" that I had purchased months before when the children painted T-shirts. I painted the words "Our Blessings Jar" on the side. I gathered the note cards that we had colored, folded them in half, and dropped each one into the jar. I tied a colorful ribbon in a bow around the lid and left it as the centerpiece on the kitchen table. And sitting next to it, I placed another stack of note cards.

The next morning the children gathered around the breakfast table. "What's this?" Jenna asked while opening the lid. "It's our blessings! We have a Blessings Jar! Let's see how many blessings we can think of today!" she shouted with excitement.

"You know, Daddy says that God is the one who gives the blessings. We just need to keep track of them," Jason reported.

And for the past twelve years we have. Our children now read for themselves stories of God's faithfulness to Moses, Joseph, and David. They've learned to trust when they can't see past their cocoons. They know that somehow, someway, a butterfly will emerge. And they know without a doubt who makes the butterfly fly.

Tonight I added another blessing to the Mitchell family's Blessings Jar. "Lord," I wrote, "thanks for the dark nights when challenges knocked on our door like a regular visitor. Thanks for the special note cards and crayons. And thanks for giving us a way to read about your faithfulness to the Mitchells!"

When Jenna and Joel had their medical crises, Janet and Marty focused completely on their needs. Janet commented, "Even though I counted heads and all three of my children were accounted for, four-year-old Jason, my typical child without special needs, had needs that were going unmet. All my time, attention, and energy were directed toward the crises at hand. With thirteen hospitalizations that first year, nothing in our home was normal. Once I realized I needed help, I called in the troops—family and friends who volunteered to take shifts at the hospital just so Jason and I could spend time together. Once we brought Jenna and Joel home, these special caregivers continued this routine, making sure Jason and I had 'Mommy and me' time."

Jason loved the time and attention he received. He also prided himself on being the big brother who knew to shake his baby brother if and when the heart monitor alarmed. He felt important when he was taught how to dial those important numbers—911. Jason was thriving, and he cherished his brother and sister.

Judy Dunning shares a story about her daughters, Brooke and Paige. Brooke's situation is similar to Jason's. She, too, exhibits a special kind of love for her sister in "Aren't We Lucky."

Aren't We Lucky
JUDY DUNNING

My dreams for my children were for them to be happy, healthy individuals who would grow to be thoughtful, caring adults with something to offer this world. In addition to my hopes and dreams for the future, I had a mental picture of how our family would look.

My so-called picture changed in January 1997, the day my second daughter, Paige, was born.

After an uneventful but overdue second pregnancy, my uterus ruptured during early labor. I had been induced while attempting a regular delivery, even though my first daughter, Brooke, had been delivered by C-section two years before. Paige was delivered and resuscitated, but she had experienced oxygen loss that caused a brain injury. After a five-week stay in the hospital's NICU, Paige was discharged and later diagnosed with cerebral palsy.

Paige is now a beautiful and healthy five-year-old. She has developmentally progressed slowly but has not experienced plateaus in any area yet. Instead of comparing her to other children her age, I look at this process as a slow recovery from an injury. Adopting this attitude has helped me maintain an optimistic, yet realistic, viewpoint. It also has given me better endurance for the long road ahead.

Developmentally, Paige is still working on the big stuff, like head control, rolling, sitting, and all other gross and fine motor skills. But through it all, we've thoroughly enjoyed her presence. She is a happy, patient, and loving little girl with a cute sense of humor. She adores movies, books, and music. She enjoys being tickled and likes lots of cuddling. She communicates with her eyes and facial expressions and has taught all of us about life and love. Paige has had the comfort of a loving family, a dog who can't stay away from her, and the unconditional love of her seven-year-old sister, Brooke.

One day, as Brooke was sitting in Paige's room, she asked if she could rock her sister. I propped Paige in her arms, and Brooke said, "Mom, aren't we lucky Paige is taking longer to grow up than other kids?"

"Why?" I asked.

"Because we get to hold her for a little bit longer."

How right Brooke is. We are lucky—and blessed!

True love does not come by finding the perfect person but by learning to see an imperfect person perfectly.
—JASON JORDAN

Chapter 3

LOVING UNCONDITIONALLY

The Elephant Ear

MARTI KRAMER-SUDDARTH

Alex's face brightened when he entered the garden. His great-grandpa chuckled as Alex made a beeline to the watering can and then headed for the elephant ear plant.

At three years old, Alex seldom made eye contact and spoke only two words. He paced, refused to use utensils when eating, and lined up his toys rather than playing with them. When frustrated, Alex beat his head on the floor, bruising his forehead in the process. A local psychologist suspected autism.

Alex had few social connections. He didn't know how to play with the children in his church nursery and treated extended family members like pieces of scenery. His older sister handled the situation by ordering Alex around, but many other people simply walked away, satisfied when he wasn't causing trouble.

His relationship with his great-grandpa, however, was different. Great-grandpa Morris was a gardener, a man who could grow tomato vines so tall that a ladder was needed to harvest the tomatoes. Though age had trimmed the extent of his garden, it hadn't curtailed his love of the process or his ability to grow fantastic plants.

The summer Alex was diagnosed with early childhood autism, Morris grew a giant elephant ear plant. Alex and his mother often walked over to visit him while Alex's sister attended preschool. A comforting ritual evolved. Upon entering the gate, Alex headed straight for the watering can and then for the elephant ear plant, with Great-grandpa Morris following close behind. After tending to the plant, the two gardeners surveyed the rest of the vegetation, watering and weeding with care. There in the garden, great-grandfather and great-grandson found a place to connect. Through their mutual interest in the elephant ear, they were able to develop a relationship that might not otherwise have occurred.

By late fall, the elephant ear plant had grown over nine feet tall. Alex's interest grew with the plant. His great-grandpa claimed that the secret was manure, but Alex's mother knew it was his green thumb and his love of plants.

That winter Alex's father found a job out of state, and the family moved away. Visits with Great-grandpa Morris were limited, and his health began to fail. Yet a wonderful teacher began working with Alex, and he opened up to the people around him. Great-grandpa Morris died before Alex and his family were able to move back home. Though he never got to see the boy Alex would become, Great-grandpa Morris had planted a seed that would blossom.

A gardener can't see with his eyes the plant a seed will become, but he plants the seed anyway, knowing that God has great plans. To the Master Gardener, Alex was like that seed, needing just a little time and care to grow, and he knew what was to come. God gave Great-grandpa Morris a gardener's eyes, and through those eyes he saw Alex as the wonderful person he would become.

Like Great-grandpa Morris, Karen Kosman is a grandparent of a child with special needs. Karen writes the following:

I don't think anyone would argue that being a grandparent is a blessing. In Scripture, God demonstrates this truth in Proverbs 17:6: "Grandchildren are the crown of the elderly, and the pride of sons is their fathers."

God in his infinite wisdom intended for the relationship between parent, child, and grandparent to be special. A grandparent's love often makes a profound difference in a grandchild's life.

For a grandparent-to-be, those nine months of waiting become a time to share, a time of wonder, a time of hope, and a time to dream. Images of a baby boy or baby girl help to write love letters on a joyful heart. Perhaps many hours are spent praying for a healthy baby. Then something goes terribly wrong, and the news is not good. Perhaps the baby is physically or mentally handicapped, or maybe an accident or illness transforms a healthy child into a child with special needs.

Whatever the cause, human emotions emerge when grandparents are faced with the reality that their *blessing* has special needs. They sometimes try to push the truth behind a veil of denial. They struggle with grief and wonder why God would allow this pain. Sometimes grandparents' struggles include not knowing how to help. They wrestle with the desire to help but feel unsure. They fear their help may seem like interference, and self-questions are asked: "How can I help my grandchild? How can I influence my son or daughter about the child's future without interfering?" Often they worry about the added emotional and financial stress their adult child now assumes and pray that they can sustain the load.

As the next story demonstrates, love is a powerful remedy. God has woven within each human being the need to love and be loved. This miracle of God's love transfers grief into action. It is demonstrated in "The Miracle of Jay-Jay."

The Miracle of Jay-Jay
LOUISE TUCKER JONES

"He doesn't look like the other boys," Grandpa said as he viewed the blanketed bundle I held in my arms.

Grandpa was right. James Ryan, whom we called Jay-Jay, with his skinny little legs, almost bald head, and tiny up-slant eyes, bore little resemblance to the other chubby babies of mine with their full heads of hair. But I knew the comment went far beyond looks. Grandpa couldn't accept the fact that Jay-Jay had Down syndrome and was mentally challenged.

On subsequent visits Pa-Pa, the name the children used for their grandpa, ignored Jay-Jay. He picked him up once when it seemed to be expected for a family picture. Other than that he never touched him and looked upon him with something between pity and displeasure.

Then one day a miracle began. It was at a family reunion, and Jay-Jay, being the outgoing little boy he was at three years old, walked over to his grandpa and crawled onto his lap. Pa-Pa was a little shocked, but what could he do in front of all these people? This was his grandson. How could they understand that he hardly knew Jay-Jay?

Jay-Jay took Pa-Pa's glasses out of his shirt pocket and placed them on his own face, upside down, precariously perched on his short, pudgy nose. He looked at Pa-Pa and giggled, making Pa-Pa laugh too—genuinely. Soon they were walking around the room, Jay-Jay leading Pa-Pa, a little smile on the older one's face.

Their next encounter came months later when Pa-Pa decided to visit and Jay-Jay played the clown, making his grandpa laugh, pick him up, and throw him into the air.

Pa-Pa turned to my husband and said, "Why, he's just like any other kid."

We had tried to tell him, but Pa-Pa's preconceived ideas and fears of the disabled had kept him out of his grandson's life. But Jay-Jay, being an effervescent little boy, would not let him remain in darkness. With his love and actions he showed Pa-Pa and others that they were missing out on some of God's greatest blessings by not loving and caring for him.

After that day a strong bond began to form. Pa-Pa found that Jay-Jay loved balloons, so he would have one waiting for him each time we came to visit—visits he now welcomed. Then he discovered that Jay-Jay was not only sweet but ornery and loved pillow fights. So each visit would end up with pillows flying across the room. I never figured out which of the two enjoyed this time the most. Soon Pa-Pa began to telephone, supposedly to talk to my husband, who was now glowing in the new relationship between his father and his son. Yet Pa-Pa always insisted on speaking to his youngest grandson.

Although Jay-Jay has a severe speech articulation disorder, he can understand most of what is said to him. Yet he finds it difficult to form the words he wants to say, making communication difficult. Nevertheless, Pa-Pa always wanted to speak to him by phone, and

Jay-Jay would laugh and talk in words that neither his dad nor I understood. Pa-Pa swore he understood every word.

The phone chats became a weekly ritual. Every Saturday morning Jay-Jay knew it was the day to talk to Pa-Pa. Since it was long distance, they took turns calling. One week Pa-Pa would call. The next week, all excited, Jay-Jay would make the call and talk until we made him hang up.

Through the years Jay-Jay and Pa-Pa continued those weekly phone calls, along with letters, cards, fishing trips, and frequent trips to Wal-Mart. They became "best buddies." When Jay, as he is called today, was nineteen, his beloved Pa-Pa died unexpectedly. One of the most painful yet proud days of my life was watching Jay stand at Pa-Pa's graveside and received the American flag that had draped the casket. I will always cherish knowing that Jay's unconditional love built a bridge to his grandfather's heart and changed both of their worlds forever.

Our lives are forever changed when we are loved by a child with special needs. Being loved for who we are—without conditions—is refreshing. This love comes in all shapes and sizes. In fact, it comes hidden in "special" children. It might be in their laughter, in the sparkle of their eyes, or in their smiles. It may be seen through their kindness or perseverance to try and try again.

"I'm rich!" a grandpa said. "If hugs were dollars, I'd be a millionaire."

Susan, too, is rich. She has developed a relationship with her mentally challenged stepson, Rick. She has found an *unconditional* love for him, loving him through the good times as well as through difficult circumstances. Susan often reminds Rick that she is "Only a Phone Call Away."

Only a Phone Call Away
SUSAN TITUS OSBORN

When I married Dick eleven years ago, I began to look at his children and grandchildren as my own. This has been especially important to

Rick, Dick's forty-year-old mentally challenged son. Rick was born without a thyroid, which his pediatrician failed to notice during his well-baby checkups—and then it was too late. As a result, his growth is stunted, his hearing is impaired, and he functions below the typical level.

Before Dick and I married, Rick eagerly asked me, "Susan, when you marry my dad, will you become my mom?"

I replied, "Yes!" and was delighted to become Rick's mom. I have worked hard to fill that role. I love him unconditionally. To foster our relationship, Dick and I have a toll-free number he can call day or night. And he does.

Rick lives in the present, and every little incident that happens to him seems like a major crisis, so he calls. I calmly help him deal with issues such as having his bike stolen for the tenth time because he forgot to put it away. Or having someone tease him at his apartment building.

Rick lives on his own near his sister about five hours from us and enjoys his independence. Because of his handicapping condition, we are still parenting him and always will. Various family members have tried to help him take care of his financial affairs, but he refuses since he wants to "do it" by himself. Yet the checks continue to bounce, and there are always more days in a month than his SSI check can cover. Yes, Rick often reminds us that we are only a phone call away.

Because of his difficulty in processing thoughts logically, Rick becomes frustrated and angers easily, so he struggles in relationships with his family members and friends. He has been to anger management classes and is working hard on controlling his anger.

Yet Rick is loving and thoughtful. He always remembers to call me on Mother's Day, on my birthday, or just to say hi. His dad travels around the country, so Rick calls often to ask, "Where is Dad now?" When something exciting happens or he succeeds at some accomplishment, he wants Dick and me to be the first to know. He always ends his conversations with "I love you, Mom."

Like a child, he is always standing in front of his apartment building watching for us when we go to visit him. As soon as we step out of the car, he rushes to his dad and me and gives us bear hugs. He always has a big smile and is thrilled to see us.

Through Rick's childlike sensitivity and exuberant expressions,

I know I am loved. I am confident Rick and I will always love each other unconditionally.

Many of us have never experienced someone loving us unconditionally. How wonderful it must feel for Rick to know that no matter how many mistakes he makes, how many crises he has, or how many times he calls—Susan is there for him.

Janet says, "Susan's love for Rick demonstrates to me the love Jesus has for us. No matter how many mistakes we make, how many crises we face, or how many times we call on him for help—Jesus is there for us."

Nanette Thorsen-Snipes discovered this unconditional love one cold winter day. She shares her story in "A Splash of Sunshine."

A Splash of Sunshine
NANETTE THORSEN-SNIPES

The joyful effect of a smile is something I learned to appreciate as I grew older. I had no idea what effect a smile, the only ray of light some people see all week, could have on others. A friendship developed through one such smile with a grocery-store bagger named Matt, a young man with Down syndrome.

One particularly cold and wintry day, I drove to the grocery store. I watched the wind whip the pine trees, bending them nearly to the ground. The snow clouds, heavy and dark, stood ready to birth new snow. My body ached from arthritis, and when I emerged from my car, I hobbled toward the store.

Inside, I trudged up and down each aisle like an old woman, my legs and feet stiff. The pain accompanied me to the checkout stand, where I paid for the groceries. As I pushed my cart toward the door, I noticed that Matt was watching me. With a determined look on his face, he left his post so he could help.

He pushed my cart out to the car. I stood shivering by the car door as Matt handed me the bread, which I put in the front seat. Then Matt handled my groceries with care, as though each package was the most important one in the world, while he slowly laid them on the backseat.

Snowflakes began settling on Matt's coat and hair. I was impressed by this thoughtful young man who showed such concern.

Reaching into my purse for my usual dollar tip, I realized I had spent my last dollar at the post office purchasing stamps. I fished around in the bottom of the purse, but I'd cleaned it out earlier, so I found no change.

Embarrassed by my thoughtlessness, I said, "Matt, I'm sorry, but I don't have a tip to give you."

He smiled and said, "That's OK." Unexpectedly, Matt wrapped his arms around me and lightly kissed my cheek. "I love you," he whispered.

"I'll make it up to you next time, Matt," I promised. Standing in the cold with my back aching and my fingers numb, I realized my heart was warmed by the love he openly shared. What perfect joy he poured into my day. I knew that Matt's love was like God's love—unconditional.

I left with a smile on my face and a warm feeling inside. And the ache in my body seemed to disappear. What a perfect splash of sunshine for my long winter's day—a ray of light from one of God's "special" children.

∞

Nanette found her heart warmed by a grocery-store bag boy. Matt's spontaneity and his ability to express himself brought sunshine on a cold day. "Matt, I'll make it up to you," promised Nanette. And we're sure she did!

Those who love children with special needs often find themselves in situations where they are thankful—thankful for someone's understanding, thankful for a teacher who went out of her way, or thankful for a grocery bagger who helped her get her groceries to the car.

One mom says, "I keep a small package of thank-you cards in my car. Therefore I'm always ready to drop a note and simply say, 'Thanks *so* much!'" Expressing our gratitude and appreciation is important, and somehow this expression of thanks will in turn bless your child.

Not all children's behavior and actions appear as loving as Matt's. For example, children diagnosed with autism may have a different temperament than his. Marilyn Jaskulke shares her story of loving her grandson in "Grandma, You're Fired!"

Grandma, You're Fired!

MARILYN JASKULKE

"Grandma, you're fired!" nine-year-old Taylor hollered at me.

I was shocked and a little hurt. Was Taylor really speaking to me? Did he mean that? He wasn't laughing, so I guess it's no joke.

Taylor, our grandson, is a high-functioning autistic child. In his world there is only black and white—no gray. Evidently Taylor was unhappy with me, and he was telling me what he thought!

Autism is a lifelong disorder with no known medical cure. As grandparents, we were devastated and confused when we learned of Taylor's diagnosis. We knew nothing about autism, only bits and pieces about head banging and uncontrolled behavior. How could this child I'd held in my arms and sung his favorite "Barney" song to be regressing into someone whose world would be completely different from that of our other ten grandchildren?

We agonized over Taylor's difficulties of the day and his challenges for the future. We prayed to God that he would show us how to have a relationship with Taylor. We prayed that Taylor would return our love as grandparents, that he would show a powerful need to be loved as well as a capability to love.

When Taylor was about three years old, we first sensed something was wrong. Upon driving into our kids' driveway, we could see Taylor standing at the window watching us. We expected him to be jumping up and down as he had in the past, but he showed no emotion upon seeing us arrive.

I turned to my husband and asked, "Why isn't he excited to see us?"

It wasn't until sometime later that we learned of the diagnosis of autism. "No cure. Learn to live with it" were the harsh words that came from a professional. Grief, anger, sadness, and worry filled our hearts and minds.

It took time, but gradually God revealed Taylor's potential to us. Daily we are now recognizing the love of God in everything he has given us, Taylor included.

Today Taylor is in the fourth grade. With the help of a teacher's aide, he is doing well in school. The *thump, thump, thump* of his body jumping up and down on the trampoline in his bedroom suggests he needs to be alone to unwind for a while after school. Some of his pent-up energy is crying to be released before he starts his homework.

After-school aides help keep him on track with math and reading. Cries of "No! No! I'm not going to do homework" sometimes fill the kitchen where he is seated at the table. Yet Taylor loses the battle most of the time.

Children with autism are easily upset by changes in routines. The stress leads to anger that is extremely difficult for them to control. Thus, a rigid after-school schedule is important.

We are proud of our son and daughter-in-law for all they have done to keep structure and balance in their family life and for giving their best to our grandson.

Over time I have learned what Taylor meant when he said, "Grandma, you're fired." He was frustrated with me for wanting him to do something he had no interest in doing. I've also learned that when Taylor fires someone, it means that person's firmness is good for him. Like most kids he is struggling for his own independence.

Through all Taylor's frustrations, God's unconditional love is present, reminding him in a gentle whisper, "I love you, Taylor."

"You're fired," and "I love you." Could they have the same meaning? Taylor has taught me that they do.

Most autistic children have a difficult time expressing themselves, and Taylor is no exception. Yet the people in Taylor's life have spent time learning to read beyond what he says. They realize "being fired" might not be so bad after all.

Marilyn's son and daughter-in-law have done an outstanding job of providing a structured home for Taylor. They spent time researching and learned all they could about autism. Taylor's parents are prepared for those situations in which Taylor behaves inappropriately in public. When (not if) this happens, they appropriately deal with Taylor and then use it as an educational experience for those standing by watching. Sometimes without saying a word, one of them reaches into a pocket and pulls out a card that resembles a business card. Taylor's parents have had cards printed for just this occasion. They are cutely decorated and say:

YOU HAVE JUST ENCOUNTERED
A person with an autism spectrum disorder.
He may be acting in an unusual way.
Please be understanding!
Autism is a developmental disorder that
prevents individuals from behaving in a typical manner.
http://www.autism-society.org

Taylor's parents have experienced a favorable response from those who've received one of their special cards. They've found that a little education helps to relieve many stressful moments.

Jeanne Pallos found it helpful when education and understanding were brought to her neighborhood by a mother who had the "Courage to Share."

Courage to Share

JEANNE PALLOS

When a young couple with a two-year-old moved onto our street, they seemed the perfect family. Timmy, the toddler, played in the front yard under the watchful eye of his mother. Yet, unlike other children in the neighborhood, Timmy went to physical therapy and numerous doctor appointments every week.

Not wanting to seem rude, I watched from a distance and did not ask questions. Then Timmy's mother, Lee Ann—a cheerful, energetic, positive woman—opened her heart and invited the neighborhood into her life by sending a letter explaining Timmy's condition.

Dear Neighbors,
We knew something was wrong with Timmy from the beginning. As a baby, Timmy cried all the time and began having hundreds of seizures every day. My husband and I knew parenting shouldn't be this hard.

After numerous tests, the doctors finally diagnosed Timmy with tuberous sclerosis, a disease that causes hundreds of tumors to grow in the brain and other parts of the body. Timmy is also autistic. . . .

Not only did Lee Ann tell us about Timmy; she also invited us to make a difference by supporting the Tuberous Sclerosis Foundation. I pulled out my checkbook and sent a donation.

Lee Ann, a woman of courage and openness, allowed strangers to become part of her world. She let us share Timmy's struggles and his victories. She taught us to understand, not pity, her family's special challenges.

I am thankful that Lee Ann had the courage to share. Her letters to the neighbors not only served as an educational tool, but to me it was an invitation to a friendship that I pray lasts a lifetime.

Lee Ann had a choice. She could have built walls of bitterness and self-pity around herself. Instead, she chose to educate her friends and neighbors and allow them to surround her family with love, support, and understanding. Lee Ann took a risk, and by her courage to share, she found her neighbors were willing to hold not only her hand but also her heart.

Karen Kosman also had a choice: to keep searching for the cause behind her son's slow speech development and coordination problems or to give up. After all, their pediatrician said, "Nothing is wrong," but her heart screamed that he was wrong. Turning to God, Karen prayed, "Lord, I need answers. Robbie may be different, but to me he is dear. He deserves the best in life. We need someone who understands and can help us find the right answers." God answered that prayer with a special teacher and her unconditional love in "Love and an Old Typewriter."

Love and an Old Typewriter
KAREN KOSMAN

"I don't want to go to school," my seven-year-old son whimpered. I smiled and tried one more time to get the cowlick on the back of his head to lie down.

"Robbie, you're going to like your new teacher, make new friends, and have fun in second grade."

He looked down at his feet and pouted.

Linda came rushing out of her room. "Look, Mommy, I have my new dress on." My five-year-old daughter eagerly waited to start school.

Life for my children seemed so different. Linda loved school and learned quickly.

Robbie had been diagnosed with a learning disability. Before he started school, we'd enrolled him in speech therapy. He'd improved tremendously until he started kindergarten. Then he regressed. Multiple problems developed. Coordination problems, impulsiveness, and a short attention span made him disruptive in class. He'd had to repeat kindergarten. In the first grade other kids started to label him as dumb. Every day he'd come home, and in his eyes I'd see a hurt too deep for crying.

Now in the second grade, he'd be in a smaller classroom with other "special" kids. In special education he'd receive the individual attention he needed.

As we climbed into the car, Robbie slouched down in his seat, while Linda vibrated with enthusiasm. I thought, *I hope special education is the answer.*

At school we entered Robbie's classroom. Mrs. Hanson greeted us. The classroom atmosphere communicated a sense of well-being. Bright colored posters hung on the walls. The science corner displayed a poster of the human skeleton. In another corner stood paint easels, and a color chart was on the wall. There wasn't a corner that didn't have something of interest visible.

Robbie went over to a table where an old typewriter sat. Mrs. Hanson walked up to him and said, "Robbie, would you like to type your name?"

He grinned and nodded his head. His eyes danced with excitement.

I glanced around the room. Every child seemed occupied with a project. I slipped out of the room as Mrs. Hanson sat down at the typewriter with Robbie.

One month later Mrs. Hanson held a special conference for parents. We each sat at our child's desk. I looked through Robbie's folders: art, math, and spelling—all created within the first month.

Mrs. Hanson smiled and said, "In my class children learn. Long before special education classrooms, I had to develop a program to help my own son—a child with special needs. Each item in this classroom has a function—like the old typewriter. Using it, the children learn their alphabet and improve hand-eye coordination at the same time. Plus, they love typing. Remember that children with learning disabilities are not dumb. They just learn differently."

Mrs. Hanson not only helped her students; she also taught their parents. She helped us see the potential that each of our children has.

After that first day of school, Robbie never again said, "I don't want to go to school." He eagerly looked forward to going. Robbie learned that he loved to paint and build things. He learned about tools and their proper use. He learned about the human body. He learned the alphabet and kept a notebook of short stories he and his classmates wrote. He gained confidence, and his speech pattern improved.

As a professional teacher, Mrs. Hanson helped her students academically, but she added a special ingredient called *love*. She helped them to develop character and insight that ultimately shaped their individual potential. In her class Robbie developed skills that he has never lost.

God is there turning the pages of our lives with His finger on every moment. He loves us that much.
—SHERWOOD E. WIRT

Chapter 4
TRUSTING IN SPITE OF . . .

Big Bad Bullies
DANDI DALEY MACKALL

I knew something was wrong as soon as my daughter, Katy, took her first step out of the school building. She hung her head, slipped into the car, and buckled her seat belt without being told.

"How was your day, honey?" I asked cautiously.

"Fine."

Fifth grade is no picnic for any child, especially one who sticks out in class. And Katy has a rare neurological disorder that has impaired her hearing and speech. Katy's school days are seldom fine, and this day seemed less fine than most.

I started the car, the engine's rumble matching the churning inside me. As we left the parking lot in silence, Katy studied her backpack buckle.

I whispered a quick prayer, then asked, "Katy, what happened?"

Her words, and her tears, started spilling over. "Mitch stood behind me. He made fun of me. He talked funny—like me."

"Katy, I'm sorry," I said.

But Katy wasn't finished. "Then Melissa and Brianna laughed. They all laughed at me."

Katy cried harder.

I squeezed the steering wheel and said, "Katy, I love you so much, and I love the way you talk. Let's stop for ice cream on the way home."

It's tough in the school trenches. And if a student has a disability, as Katy does, it's that much harder. But even typical school-age children may find themselves targets of a bully.

My friend Linda's second-grade daughter gets teased for being overweight. Her fourth-grade son is ridiculed for wearing thick glasses. Another seventh grader refuses to participate in sports because he's not a natural athlete. He can't stand the verbal abuse when he strikes out. And another friend's daughter, Nicole, struggles with assignments. She's been labeled slow or even stupid by several of her classmates. Do they think Nicole doesn't hear their whispers?

So what's a mother to do? We pray, get the facts, and do what God leads us to do. Then we admit there's only so much we can do about the bullies of this world. Our job is to prepare and teach our own children how to deal with them.

While you may never be able to change other people's kids, when you help your child endure tough experiences, he or she grows by learning important lessons about compassion, forgiveness, and comfort in God, as well as effective survival skills.

My friend, Meg, regrets that she lost opportunities to teach her daughter, Becky, how to face bullies. Meg's goal was to fix every problem so Becky wouldn't experience pain. If Becky got left out of an overnighter, Meg called the other mom and arranged for Becky to be included. If Becky got in trouble in high school, Meg was there to defend her daughter and get the consequences lessened. Now that Becky is away at college, Meg can't fix every problem. And Becky, sheltered from problems and pain for so many years, hasn't developed problem-solving skills to handle even minor struggles.

God didn't put us in a pain-free world. Romans 5:3–5 says pain and perseverance are parts of a character-building formula: "We know that affliction produces endurance, endurance produces proven character, and proven character produces hope. This hope does not disappoint, because God's love has been poured out in our hearts through the Holy Spirit who was given to us."

If we can help our children handle bullies now, we'll equip them for a godly life later.

I wish I had a solution to the problem of Mitch teasing Katy. We prayed. My husband and I told Katy we loved her and Jesus loved her. We couldn't find an explanation for Mitch's behavior, but we prayed for him. We talked to Katy's teacher, who already was aware of the problem. She had her students switch desks, and Katy ended up several seats away from Mitch. It slowed him down, but it didn't stop him.

My husband and I coached Katy on how she could handle the situation if it came up again. We rehearsed. Dad was Mitch. Katy's sister and I were the other girls. In practice, Katy responded cheerfully to the pretend teasing. She said, "Have a nice day, Mitch. You, too, girls." Or, "Mitch, you want to come with me to speech therapy?"

Katy did fine—in practice. At school she forgot her lines. The problem ended when the school year ended. This year we hope she'll be a little better equipped.

Bully stories don't always have happy endings. Yet with Christ's help, no matter what other people's children do, our children can grow in character and in strength—and we can grow with them.

Most of us have encountered a bully at some time. For a child with special needs, however, this may occur daily. These experiences are not just challenging; they are excruciatingly painful! Katy's mom gets an A+ in how she responded to the bullies in her child's life.

Parenting is demanding for most parents, but parenting a child with special needs poses an additional set of concerns. As parents of "special" kids, we must find the balance between encouraging our children to try and knowing when to pull back. We must choose which battles to fight and then let go of those issues that steal our time, energy, and emotions. People may label us overprotective, and maybe we are. Yet we can quietly accept this label, knowing our protection is truly needed.

We draw comfort in knowing we can trust God to meet the needs of our children. God often demonstrates his creativity in how this is accomplished. Sometime he uses the guidance of a teacher, the caring heart of a schoolmate, the expertise of a medical professional, or a simple smile from a stranger. And as Janet says, "Sometimes God even uses 'A Mother's Intuition.'"

A Mother's Intuition

JANET LYNN MITCHELL

"Hi, I'm calling to cancel my son's surgery. It's schedule for next week."

"Is there a problem, Mrs. Mitchell? Does Jason have a cold?"

Oh, how could I tell her what I was really feeling? "No," I said with a pause. Stumbling for words, I tried to explain. "I'd like you to take a message for Dr. Saundars. I need to let him know that I've canceled Jason's surgery because . . . well . . . something in my heart tells me that I need to."

That something I was speaking of was the mother's intuition that God had given me. It was an answer to the prayers I had prayed, asking God for guidance concerning Jason's health care. A still, small voice within me made clear that my son's surgery must be postponed and that I needed to seek additional medical opinions for him.

Jason, my toddler, had recently undergone surgery to remove a lymph node from his neck. Afterwards, a specialist confirmed our fears—Jason had an infectious disease. For days following the surgery, IVs dripped medication into his tiny body.

Weeks later he was still on medication to make sure that the infection had not spread. At one of our follow-up appointments, Dr. Saundars told my husband and me about Jason's needed surgery. He said, "I need to go in and make sure all the infection is gone. I'll clean out his neck and the side of his face. The risk in this surgery involves damaging the nerves. The right side of Jason's face may be paralyzed as a result."

We sat in Dr. Saundars' office too stunned for words. Like a robot, I met with the nurse and scheduled the surgery as my husband entertained Jason. Once home, I fell on my bed and began to pray. I prayed continually, asking God to direct the surgeon as well as to direct my husband and me since we were the ones ultimately responsible for making the health-care decisions for our child.

"Mrs. Mitchell," Dr. Saundars' nurse said the day I called to cancel the surgery, "I'll let the doctor know you've called, and I'll cancel the surgery on the schedule."

I did it! However nervous I was, I had followed my heart!

As soon as I hung up the phone, I gathered the papers on my desk. I had spent hours on research and knew exactly which teaching hospitals I would ask to examine Jason. I set my emotions aside and dialed the number of the National Center for Infectious Disease. In minutes I was talking with a physician from the center, reading him Jason's recent lab tests.

"Ma'am, if Jason were my son, I'd let him go play ball and forget this surgery. He's going to be fine. Keep him on the medicine for six more months just to be on the safe side."

Three weeks later Jason had his first of three appointments that I had made at different teaching hospitals. "No surgery" was the consensus of the doctors at all three hospitals.

Today I think back and remember how I had prayed and then followed the intuition God had placed in my heart. I'm thankful that God gave me the courage to cancel Jason's surgery. I'm also thankful that we were able to back that decision up with second and third medical opinions for our son.

Now that Jason is a teen, we have shared with him the story behind the scar on his neck. Jason knows that a mother's intuition is a God-given gift, and he finally understands why I get goose bumps whenever I see him smile.

Just as Jason benefited from second and third medical opinions, your child may benefit as well. Through Janet's experiences she has learned that second opinions are a must. Janet says, "Always get a second opinion. *Never* accept one laboratory result or one doctor's diagnosis as fact. Never accept one doctor's surgical recommendation as the only way of regaining your child's health. *Always* get a second opinion regarding advised surgery and/or extensive medical treatment. I recommend seeking a second opinion in an entirely different laboratory and/or medical community from that of your current doctor."

Each of us has the awesome privilege of turning to the Lord, asking him for wisdom and guidance. James 1:5 states: "Now if any of you lacks wisdom, he should ask God, who gives to all generously and without criticizing, and it will be given to him." God can be trusted to answer our prayers! When we need wisdom in making wise decisions in difficult circumstances, he will generously meet our needs and those of our child.

In making medical choices and decisions for our children, we must do our homework, researching all that we can. Here are seven tips to help you.

1.   Select Your Own Doctor.

Selecting a doctor for your child is one of the most important decisions you'll ever make. Before choosing your doctor, research. Get recommendations from friends, family, and other trusted physicians. Go as far as checking his/her standing with the medical board of your state. If your medical insurance plan is managed care, request the list of prospective doctors and learn all you can about each physician so you can make an *educated choice*. Strange but true, most people spend more time and energy in selecting a car to purchase than they do in selecting a physician. When choosing a doctor, interview each one. Ask:

- What is your area of expertise?
- How long have you been practicing medicine?
- Where did they attend medical school?
- Do you have special training in managing the condition my child may have?
- Who is on call for you when you are off duty?
- In what hospitals do you have staff privileges?

Will the doctor take time to answer these questions? Are you comfortable when talking with him/her? And most importantly, does the doctor relate well to your child or teen? When selecting a physician, you may also want to consider additional factors, such as the gender and age of the physician and the languages the doctor speaks.

2.   Prepare before Your Appointment.

Before your appointment with a doctor, make a *written* list of all questions and concerns you have pertaining to your child's health. Include a list of *all* medications he or she is presently taking. This is vitally important because many children see more than one specialist, and one doctor may not be informed of a medication prescribed by another. Also include all vitamins, herbs, and other over-the-counter medications. At the appointment provide your doctor with a copy of your questions and the list of medications. Be sure to date all lists and keep a copy for your personal records.

3.   Be Assertive.

Don't be afraid or hesitant to ask your doctor the questions on your prepared list. *No* question you have is inappropriate. Explain to your physician any concerns you have. Ask to be referred to a specialist if the need arises. Despite the sense of loyalty you may feel for your doctor, it is not an act of betrayal to seek out a specialist. No doctor can be an expert in all areas!

Remember to bring a book or something to occupy your child's time while waiting for your appointment. Be patient with your doctor if he is running late. This shows that he provides the time needed to care for his patients. If your doctor doesn't listen to your concerns or take the time to answer your questions, he or she could be hazardous to your child's health!

4.   Inform the Physician of Your Child's Past Medical History.

You must make sure the doctor is aware of your child's medical history. This includes all surgeries, serious illnesses, medication allergies, or sensitivities your child may have had. Ask that the physician request your child's medical records from all previous doctors. You should also obtain a copy of past medical records.

5.   Appeal If You've Been Denied Treatment.

If your medical insurance denies a treatment that you and your doctor feel is necessary, file an appeal with your insurance company requesting an independent review. If this review is denied, you may want to contact the insurance commissioner of your state.

6.   Before Surgery, Weigh the Pros and Cons

Ask your surgeon if he or she is board certified to perform the needed procedure, how many times he or she has performed the prescribed surgery, and what his or her success and mortality rate has been. Question your physician about any possible complications or side effects that might occur as a result of the surgery. Weigh any possible complications against the option of your child not having the surgery, and then decide if the surgery is really necessary. Lastly, ask your surgeon if he or she will be conducting your child's entire operation. (In teaching hospitals, residents actually perform many of the surgeries.)

7.   Be Appreciative of Your Doctor.

Show your child's doctor respect by keeping your appointments. Follow his or her prescribed plan for your child's health care. And once in a while, drop him a note of thanks, sealed with a prayer.

Just as Jason in the last story needed a second opinion regarding his medical crisis, Michelle's teacher also needed to find another way to meet Michelle's needs. With much creativity she did just that. Susan shares her cousin Michelle's story in "The Little Brown Bunny."

The Little Brown Bunny
SUSAN TITUS OSBORN

Sensing that something was wrong, Michelle's mom, Nancy, went to her kitchen cabinet, pulling out pots and pans. As one-year-old Michelle played on the floor, Nancy stood behind her daughter and pounded a frying pan and saucepan together. Michelle didn't flinch; the noise did not faze her whatsoever. Dropping the pans to her side, Nancy's heart sank. Now there was no question. Something was seriously wrong with her daughter's hearing.

My cousin, Michelle, was born deaf—totally deaf in one ear and profoundly deaf in the other. Shortly after discovering Michelle's disability, her parents began to learn sign language. They taught their daughter simple signs while still voicing the words, allowing her to learn to lip-read. They also had Michelle fitted with a hearing aid that provided maximum amplification.

Through preschool and kindergarten, Michelle attended private schools with small classes where the teachers were attentive to her limitations. Then Michelle's family moved to a new community, and for the first time Michelle attended the local public school. It was a difficult transition. With the larger classroom she immediately realized her hearing limitations, and school became a chore.

"I don't want to go to school!" Michelle cried almost every day when she came home.

Nancy struggled as she watched her daughter face each day hating to go to school. *Do we make her go or let her stay home? Are the other kids making fun of her? How in the world can we make life easier for her? School has been so hard for Michelle since the move!*

For Michelle and many hearing-impaired people, one of the most difficult obstacles to overcome is figuring out who is speaking in a large group. Although Michelle was great at reading lips, she became frustrated in a large classroom. By the time she could figure out who was talking, that person would have finished his or her comment or question.

When Michelle reached third grade, her teacher, Mrs. Strom, could see that she was struggling with this problem. This delightful, grandmotherly woman with gray, wispy hair and a warm, friendly smile showed sensitivity to Michelle's needs. Mrs. Strom purchased a little, brown toy bunny that provided the needed solution.

"Children," she said to her class one day, "we have a new classroom game. Whenever you want to talk, you must be holding the little brown bunny. So, if you have something to say and would like permission to speak, raise your hand, and I'll hand you the bunny."

No one but Michelle and Mrs. Strom realized the bunny was for Michelle's benefit. And it remained their secret. Finally Michelle could identify who was speaking so she could then concentrate on lip-reading. The rest of the class simply thought Mrs. Strom had devised a fun game to keep them from all talking at once.

Through a little brown bunny and the insight of Mrs. Strom, Michelle gained the confidence she needed to feel a part of her class. She also learned that she was very special since Mrs. Strom had gone out of her way to purchase the bunny and to keep their secret.

Teachers are important not only for teaching reading, writing, and math but also in helping to build our children's self-esteem. A child who is able to learn feels successful. A child who feels successful knows that she can learn. Mrs. Strom knew this truth and found a way to help Michelle.

Not all of our children have or will have a teacher as loving and wise as Mrs. Strom. At times our children may be placed in classrooms where the student-teacher ratio or the teaching style is not conducive to their needs. As parents, we must listen to our children as well as observe and keep in contact with their teachers.

Susan Tacklind was struggling in grade school. She was frustrated with her inability to learn and began to believe that she was stupid. Her mother, Helen, saw her unhappiness and searched for a way to teach Susan. Helen soon found a way to help her daughter to learn "Today, Tomorrow, and Next Year."

Today, Tomorrow, and Next Year
HELEN TACKLIND

As Susan draped herself over the top of the recliner, her legs dangled on the back side, swinging back and forth in constant motion. The blonde curls on her head cascaded down the front of the recliner while her face scrunched up in concentration as she tried to memorize her list of spelling words.

I'd raised two other children, so as Susan's mother, I realized something wasn't quite right. It shouldn't have been such an effort for Susan to learn those simple spelling words. I knew she was bright, but I also knew learning was extremely challenging for her.

I contemplated homeschooling, but I believed her teacher that year was one of the best in the school. Who was I to compete with her?

One day I volunteered to help in Susan's classroom. When I arrived, I was surprised to see that my daughter wasn't in the room. "Where is Susan?" I asked.

"Susan's in the hall," Mrs. Wilson replied.

I looked quizzically at her and then followed her into the hall. There Susan sat at a desk, being overseen by a teacher's aide as she finished an art project.

Mrs. Wilson said, "Susan is my messy student, so that's why I've got her out here in the hall."

Upon hearing those words, the aide cringed, her face mirroring my exact thoughts. I was totally shocked! I wanted to cry. My decision to homeschool Susan the following year was made in that instant.

Homeschooling solved many problems for my daughter, but it created a new set of problems for me as I prepared to teach the fourth grade. I gave up my own creative projects, personal freedom, and volunteer work—where I could make or do something and see immediate results—for this new endeavor. At first I felt frustrated because my efforts didn't appear successful. Yet I knew that Susan had to be homeschooled, and God was calling me to this task.

One night, after working on her multiplication tables, I tucked Susan into bed. Clearly upset, she confided, "Mom, I know I knew my multiplication tables yesterday, but I don't know them today. I must be stupid."

My heart went out to my daughter. I had no idea she struggled so hard. "Susan, you are a very bright girl. I'm glad I'm your teacher now. We'll find a way for you to learn your multiplication tables so you will know them today, tomorrow, and next year."

In spite of my words, teaching Susan didn't seem to get any easier. I'd give her an assignment, and it seemed to take twice as long as it should to complete it—if she even understood it and did the work at all.

The following week I went to a luncheon for homeschool moms. One mom talked about her son and the problems he faced overcoming a learning disability. For a moment I was confused. It seemed as if she were talking about Susan, for Susan experienced similar challenges. I then wondered if Susan, too, had a learning disability. Since she could read, I hadn't thought this to be a possibility.

My conversation with that mom opened a door to a better understanding of my daughter. She gave me hope and told me where Susan could find help.

I had Susan tested, and she was diagnosed with a learning disability. With proper learning techniques she eventually was able to memorize, spell, and retain. She also learned her multiplication tables.

Susan has made unbelievable progress. Today my daughter is a beautiful, outgoing young woman and a high school graduate. Throughout her last nine years of schooling, I was her teacher, and all the time I spent instructing her was worthwhile. God gave me the courage to take Susan out of public school and be her teacher at a time when my daughter's needs were so great. I offered her all that I could— and that was me.

As Helen discovered, life does change after a child is diagnosed with special needs. Janet says, "When Jenna was first diagnosed with diabetes, a doctor sounded convincing when he said, 'Yes, your daughter's going to be insulin dependent, but Jenna can live a *normal* life.'

"I'd like to see this doctor again and let him know that after living twelve years with diabetes, there is nothing *normal* about it! There's absolutely nothing normal about setting a kitchen timer in the wee hours of the night, fearful that we might sleep through Jenna's needed blood sugar test. There is nothing normal about waiting for a prescription, then dealing with the insurance company because Jenna's monthly allotment of insulin was dropped and shattered into pieces. There is nothing normal in raising a teenager who is striving to become independent while I sit at home begging God to remind her not to eat the junk food at our church's youth night and pleading with him to remind her to take her last shot of the day!

"I now know that when a child is diagnosed with special needs, the life the child and family once knew will change. For many of us change is scary, and we resist it as best we can. Yet I believe the sooner change is made and expectations are appropriately realigned, the quicker the child and his or her family will find a new normalcy. It's now normal for Marty and me to wake in the middle of the night and check on Jenna. It's now normal for me to carry a backpack in the trunk of my car with an emergency supply of Jenna's shots, insulin, apple juice, and food. It's normal for me to have these same supplies packed away in my earthquake kit and at Jenna's school—just in case. It's normal for me to expect a phone call from Jenna at any time of the day, saying that she needs my help. It's normal for Jenna to attend school for two and a half hours a day and then have a homeschool teacher one day a week. And due to Jenna's unusual schedule, it's normal for my dad and Jenna to have a weekly lunch date!"

This new normalcy will include repeated medical challenges, hospitalizations, therapy appointments, disappointments, and continuous assessment of goals. Janet and her family will continue to have crises; they are simply expected.

James 1:2–3 says, "Consider it a great joy, my brothers, whenever you experience various trials, knowing that the testing of your faith produces endurance." Note that this Scripture does not say *if* but *when*. Trials *will* come our way. The great joy we are to experience comes from knowing that God is in control. Waves will come to rock our boats, but God has asked parents of children with special needs to step out into the deep waters of trust. Waves will continue to toss and turn us, but way down deep the ocean is still.

Sarah's mom has experienced God's faithfulness through the storms in her life. She's trusted him to meet her daughter's needs, needs she could never have attempted to meet by herself. She rejoices with God as he truly gave her "A Night to Remember."

A Night to Remember
SARAH'S MOM

My heart ached as day after day I watched my daughter, Sarah, sitting by the phone waiting for an invitation to her high school prom. *Why wouldn't she want to go?* I thought. *It's her last year of high school, and she's never been to a dance.*

Each day Sarah sat with anticipation, while my hope began to waver. I had held Sarah in my arms as she faced many disappointments. Yet this time I had no idea how I would pick up the pieces of my daughter's broken heart.

"Who would take a wheelchair-bound gal to a dance?" I asked Neil, a trusted family friend from the single-parent group of my church. Fighting tears, I continued, "All Sarah wants is to feel that she belongs. All I really need is one precious boy who, for a night, could look past my daughter's *chair* and into her heart."

"I understand," Neil said while nodding his head in agreement. "If that phone call doesn't come through, let me know."

The phone call that Sarah anticipated never arrived, but one from Neil did. A few days before the prom, my daughter and I were acting like schoolgirls as we weaved in and out of the stores, buying just the right dress.

"Mom, look at these heels," Sarah marveled. "Just because I can't walk doesn't mean I can't wear heels. They'll match the dress perfectly."

The big night came. Sarah's day at the salon was a hit as her hair was neatly curled and placed in an up-do. Her nails were polished. She looked beautiful in her dress and matching shoes as she waited for Neil. For that night Neil would escort my daughter to dinner and the Pantages Theater to see a play. Meanwhile, I would bake cookies with his three young boys.

Instead of a precious high school boy seeing the needs of my daughter's heart, Neil looked into my heart and then gave my daughter what I could not. What Sarah really wanted was a chance to feel special and beautiful. What I so desired was for the right guy to do just that! And my prayers were answered.

Sarah felt beautiful the night she and Neil went on their special "date." Her inward beauty was magnified by her smile. It truly was a night to remember, for that night Sarah began believing that one day a boy could look beyond her chair and into her heart.

Karen Kosman says, "God sees beyond any physical deformity to the beauty within us. So is God really saying no if the prayed-for miracle never materializes? Perhaps the *true miracle* is when hope and faith remain even in the midst of tears and disappointment—and when the human heart accepts God's sovereignty."

Karen Ruhle shares her *true miracle*, for she says, "Every Day Is a Miracle."

Every Day Is a Miracle

KAREN RUHLE

My whole world came apart in an instant. I walked out of the doctor's office with my heart pounding. I had just been given a death sentence for my baby.

"Just how will I break this news to my husband?" I cried as I fastened Karlson in his car seat. Would I factually report, "Our son has been diagnosed with SMA, spinal muscular atrophy, the largest genetic killer of children under the age of two," or would I scream, "Our baby is going to die"? Driving home, the doctor's chilling words rebounded in my mind: "We don't expect Karlson to live past a year."

My husband, Karl, was speechless when I told him the devastating news. With his own health problems and recent kidney transplant, he couldn't cope. I, on the other hand, pulled myself together the best I could. Fighting grief over what could have been, I made a commitment to Karlson. I promised him that I would make the best of each day that we had together. This meant that there would be little time for pity parties. I wanted to be able to look back and know that I had done everything I could for my son.

Soon Karlson needed a tracheostomy and was placed on a ventilator. A feeding tube was required because he could no longer swallow. How I missed cradling him and giving him a bottle. Then Karlson got pneumonia, his lungs collapsed, and he fought to live. Through Halloween, Thanksgiving, Christmas, and his birthday, he was hospitalized.

Not knowing the prescription for parenting a terminally ill child, I clung to Isaiah 41:10: "So do not fear, for I am with you; do not be dismayed, for I am your God. I will strengthen you and help you; I will uphold you with my righteous right hand" (NIV).

Since that day when we received his death sentence, I have learned to depend completely on God's strength. Karlson is now five. He likes to sing and interact with people. He loves art projects and knows his colors, shapes, and even the alphabet. He's very bright. He looks forward to working with his teacher, who comes and homeschools him five hours a week.

Karlson has beat the odds and outlived his life expectancy. Still wheelchair bound, on a ventilator, and using a feeding tube, his belly laugh turns heads. With each passing year our church celebrates his birthday with a celebration-of-life party. We use this occasion as a fund-raiser to raise money for families with SMA kids and to help find a cure for this disease. Even the local firemen, who have repeatedly come to Karlson's rescue, have attended these parties.

Karlson understands that he has special needs, and yet he still has desires to do what typical children like to do. About a year ago Karlson wanted to enter the Hawaiian Tropics Beauty Pageant. He was the first disabled child to participate. We bought him the perfect outfit and gelled his hair.

When it was his turn, he was lifted onstage and received deafening applause. "Go, Karlson. Yea, Karlson," the crowd screamed. The more they cheered, the bigger he smiled. I held his arm up at the elbow so he could wave. There wasn't a dry eye in the house. Proudly he accepted prizes for first runner-up, best hair, and best smile.

The Marines were there representing Toys for Tots. Karlson was thrilled when he was made an honorary Marine. The local paper captured the moment, which brought additional public awareness of SMA.

For the past five years my purpose has been to care for Karlson. In many ways I feel my life is on hold. I don't get enough sleep, and I burn out. I've given up my job and life as I knew it. Sometimes I wonder what my purpose in life will be once Karlson is gone. When these thoughts come, I remind myself, "So do not fear, for I am with you" (Isa. 41:10 NIV). I choose to trust God in spite of fears about losing my son.

Today I feel truly blessed that God chose me to be Karlson's mother. I am thankful that I have been able to share these years with him. Each day has been a miracle. I know that I couldn't manage what is required of me without my relationship with Jesus Christ. He has sustained me. He has carried me, and he gives me hope for tomorrow. For I know—without a doubt— that I will see my son again. We will spend eternity together!

Like Karen, many of us have learned what it means to trust God with the details of our lives. We've learned that we can depend on him in spite of our circumstances and in spite of our pain and sorrow. We've learned that trusting is a choice, a decision that is ours alone to make.

Janet says, "I've had times in my life when I've asked, 'Do I trust you, Lord?' Each time this question has crossed my mind I have come to the conclusion, 'Yes, I Trust You, Lord!'"

Yes, I Trust You, Lord!

JANET LYNN MITCHELL

Do I trust you, Lord,
When my clenched jaws ache,
And my child's diagnosis makes my heart break?
    Do I trust you, Lord,
    When my dreams have died,
    And I can't count the tears I have cried?
        Do I trust you, Lord,
        When my child's in pain,
        And my efforts to help are in vain?

Yes, I trust you, Lord,
Though the future looks bleak,
And my much-needed strength is too weak.
    Yes, I trust you, Lord,
    When I can't see your plan,
    And as hard as I try, I don't understand.
        Yes, I trust you Lord,
        Even when your answers are no,
        I'll brace myself and depend on you so.

Yes, I trust you, Lord,
Even though I'm blinded by fear,
And despite my wishing, I don't feel you near.
    Yes, I trust you, Lord,
    And I'll cling to your Word
    And know that my prayers you have heard.
        Yes, I trust you, Lord,
        To help me to be
        To this child the loving parent that you are to me!

> *He who cannot forgive breaks the bridge over*
> *which he himself must pass.*
> —GEORGE HERBERT

Chapter 5

FORGIVING THE UNFORGIVABLE

When Your Best Isn't Good Enough

SYLVIE HESTER

Life was hard. Two years had passed since our eight-year-old Amy's pancreas had completely stopped producing insulin. Predictable reactions to the doctor's formula for balancing medication, activities, and food were now a vague memory. No matter how often Amy tested—six, eight, or ten finger pokes a day—no matter how much we counted carbohydrates and adjusted the combination of fast- and slow-acting insulin, and no matter how much we prayed, Amy's blood sugar readings continued to bounce all over the place.

Each evening I tensed when my anxious husband arrived home from work and asked the same question, "What are Amy's blood sugar readings?"

"How is Amy feeling?" The dreaded question prefaced almost every telephone conversation with friends and family.

"When does Amy get out of the hospital this time?" inquired

concerned but impatient teachers, school friends, and neighborhood playmates.

"If you prayed more, your daughter wouldn't still be diabetic," a self-righteous young Christian mom said to me in the grocery store checkout line.

"Prayed more!" I wanted to scream. "No one could ever pray more than I have!"

Through tears, I tossed my groceries into the trunk of my car and drove home.

As a mom, I felt overwhelmed and inadequate in my inability to help my daughter. My entire life revolved around Amy's erratic blood sugar readings and their effect on the well-being of my beloved oldest daughter.

Amy's bedroom housed a menagerie of donated stuffed animals, but all too often it lacked a human occupant. I spent hours at her hospital bedside, praying that IV needles would go into tiny dehydrated veins, nagging harried nurses to deliver medication on time, and conferring with doctors about test results and insulin dosage changes. When possible, I encouraged the completion of homework and commiserated with parents of other sick children.

After being interrogated by every prospective intern and doctor within the first few hours of yet another hospital admission, I was in no mood to go over all the gory details one more time.

Trying to smile, I breezed by the counselor seated in the corridor. She, however, wouldn't be ignored. I froze at the first words out of her mouth: "How does it feel to do everything right and have everything go wrong? You know, some things are simply out of your control."

I turned around and faced her. "What? You mean I'm doing something right?" I blurted out with relief. "So, tell me why! Why, if I'm doing everything right, is everything going wrong?"

Immediately I began to cry. My bottled-up tears of inadequacy, fear, and exhaustion flowed freely. I slumped into a chair beside her and basked in the few moments of TLC that I so desperately needed. This counselor's kindness and words of insight gave me what I needed to face another grueling day. She skillfully soothed my wounded spirit. With a few words she restored my hope and faith in myself.

"How does it feel to do everything right and have everything go wrong?" Her words echoed in my mind.

It feels great knowing that I'm doing something right! And it feels great knowing I can trust God to tend to everything that goes wrong.

∽

Sometimes those of us who love children with special needs expect too much of ourselves. Like Amy's mother, we might feel responsible to control situations that are out of our control. Rest assured that there is no perfect family—no perfect mother who has mastered each and every detail in caring for her child with special needs and no perfect father balancing the jobs of father, supportive husband, and employee.

Sometimes, because of our high expectations of ourselves, we may even develop the idea that our frustrations and anger are ungodly, and any feeling or display of them would disappoint God. What we often forget is that God created us with human emotions.

Author Norman Wright says, "The experience of anger is normal and natural. As part of being made in God's image, humans have emotions, and one of those emotions is anger. Like all of God's gifts, anger has tremendous potential for good. We can choose to express our anger in ways that help or in ways that hinder, in ways that build or in ways that destroy."

"So it is OK to be angry?" one mother asked. "You mean it's OK to be angry that my child is suffering, and it's OK to be angry with the people who inconsiderately gawk and stare at my child?"

Yes, and being told that we shouldn't be angry is nonsense. Often, facing our anger and allowing ourselves to feel are the first steps in resolving our anger.

Judy Winter has found that helping to educate others is a way of using anger for good. She shares her story in "A Thoughtless Comment."

A Thoughtless Comment
JUDY WINTER

I stood beside my son in the frozen-food aisle of our favorite grocery store, trying to decide between Double Chocolate Chunk and Mackinac Island Fudge ice cream, when a woman suddenly appeared and quickly stole our playful mood.

"What's wrong with him?" she rudely inquired, as her young daughter perched precariously on the back of their overflowing grocery cart.

The "him" she referred to was my twelve-year-old son, Eric, whose cerebral palsy required the use of a wheelchair. The question was intrusive and demanding, and the stranger who asked it wore a pained expression that said more than her stinging words ever could convey.

It wasn't the first time I'd been asked this question. After a decade of parenting a child with cerebral palsy, I've discovered that many people are surprised to learn that people with disabilities move among us. A happy, attractive, and well-adjusted child with special needs creates an image they can't easily digest. Unfortunately for my son, these individuals usually avoided looking into his eyes and speaking to his wheelchair in order to maintain the distorted image they held of the disabled.

"There's nothing wrong with him," I said honestly, offering a brief explanation of Eric's special needs.

"It's a shame, because he's so cute," she responded before delivering her final blow. "I don't think I could stand having a handicapped child." Then she turned and walked away.

I shook my head at the intrusion that threatened the priceless moments of normalcy I'd created for my son. It's tough to parent a child with a disability, but negative societal reactions make it much tougher. Appearing in public with a wheelchair user invites unwelcome stares and thoughtless comments not only from curious children but also from adults who should know better. We face significant daily challenges—from handicapped parking violators to educational roadblocks to blatant discrimination. Still, nothing stings more than the unwanted attention of strangers loudly misjudging my child.

Yet when it comes to my son, I don't feel shortchanged. In all his glorious imperfection, Eric was my greatest life teacher. He taught me to elevate parenting above career and self-interest, to judge less, and to forgive more. He solidified my faith in God, increasing my sense of wonder at God's faithfulness and his remarkable blessings.

Eric taught me to listen when communication goes beyond words. His physical challenges demanded that I stop long enough to savor shooting stars and fireball sunsets. He's made me a more honest journalist, and when he struggled to say "I love you," he commanded center stage.

I used to sneak into his room late at night to marvel at his perfect body in slumber. It was the only time I pretended things were different.

I can't imagine having a better son.

The woman in the grocery store wasn't the first to rudely intrude upon my day, and she wasn't the last. Usually I welcome a stranger's questions as an important opportunity to educate the public about individuals with disabilities and to share my incredible faith journey. But sometimes, like everybody else, I just want to buy ice cream.

[Shortly after this was written, Eric unexpectedly passed away.]

Judy is not alone. All of us who love children with special needs have encountered people who are rude and thoughtless. At times we want to cover our child's ears so they might be spared hearing an impulsive comment or an uneducated statement. We all find ourselves with opportunities to forgive and forgive again.

Jesus said it best in Luke 23:34 as he hung from the cross—mocked, spit upon, and racked with pain: "Father, forgive them, because they do not know what they are doing."

Forgiveness is not just a gift that we give others but a gift we give ourselves. It is realizing that to err is human and that we all fall short. Forgiving releases energy for good that might otherwise be bottled with anger. We relax clenched fists, forget the injury, and move on. Forgiveness is giving to others what God has given us.

"There's one person I thought I could never forgive," one mother wrote. "I was certain that this person was somehow to blame for my child's birth defect. However hard it would be, I knew I had to face her; I had to face *myself* and forgive." This mother shares her story in "The Ultimate Payback."

The Ultimate Payback

A MOTHER

When I first learned of my baby's special needs, I felt angry. I wanted to place blame. Motionless, I stood in front of a mirror staring at my body, wondering if it were my genes that had caused her disabilities.

I mentally reviewed my family's medical history, and everything seemed to check out fine. Quickly I reminded myself of all I had done to maintain my health during my pregnancy. I had even quit drinking soft drinks and made sure I got plenty of sleep.

After another glance in the mirror, I paused. I looked deep into my own eyes. Immediately I began to make a list of the sins of my past. I tallied the score. "It is your fault!" I screamed at the reflection in the mirror. "If only I hadn't. . . . If only I had . . . my baby might be whole today." I cried as my body dropped to the floor. "*God*, why are you punishing a precious baby? It's me you should punish. I should have to live with the results of my sin! This is truly the ultimate payback!"

Only seconds passed before my own thoughts collided with my convictions. How could I forget what I know in my heart to be true? How could I allow my pain to rally my emotions and come to such conclusions?

With a sense of urgency I pulled myself from the floor and headed for my Bible. With my voice vibrating in motion with my hands, I began to recite 1 John 1:9, a verse I had memorized as a child: "If we confess our sins, He is faithful and righteous to forgive us our sins and to cleanse us from all unrighteousness."

Flipping the pages through Scripture, I turned to Isaiah 1:18. I wept tears of joy as I read: "'Come now, let us reason together,' says the LORD. 'Though your sins are like scarlet, they shall be as white as snow; though they are red as crimson, they shall be like wool'" (NIV).

I spent the next hour curled up on my couch reading. God's Word made it clear. My daughter's disabilities are not the result of my *forgiven* or *unforgiven* sins. For I believe in a God who has already provided payment for my past, present, and future sins through the sacrifice of his Son, Jesus. Through Scripture God also reminded me that he himself had formed my child in my womb, and marvelous are his works.

The mother in "The Ultimate Payback" asked the piercing question: "What did I do to cause my child's disability?"

During Jesus' time on earth, his disciples presented the same question in John 9:2 when they met a man who had been blind from birth: "Rabbi, who sinned, this man or his parents, that he was born blind?"

Jesus answered in verse 3: "Neither this man sinned nor his parents. . . . This came about so that God's works might be displayed in him."

Blaming God, others, or yourself is a natural reaction to finding out your child has a disability. We want answers to our questions: Who caused this? Who is to blame?

After the initial shock and anger wear off about a child's disability, a parent begins an internal argument.

- If only I hadn't . . . maybe this wouldn't be happening.
- If only the doctors had . . .
- If only I had known, I would have . . .
- If only I'd studied our family's medical history.
- If only . . .

The mother in our story finally realized she was not responsible for her child's disability, and God was not punishing her for her past sins. With this reassurance she stopped blaming herself and thanked God for the child he had formed in her womb.

Jeanne Pallos has paraphrased Psalm 139:13–16. May God use these words to comfort your aching heart. Perhaps you'd like to make the psalm your own and substitute your child's name for the italicized phrases:

God, I want to believe you formed *my child's* inward
parts and, like a tapestry, put every detail of *my child's* being
together.

Even if I don't feel it, I thank you for making *my child*
in such a wonderful way. Even with *my child's* special needs,
I marvel at *my child's* life.

Before the ultrasound could see *my child*, you knew every
detail of *my child's* life.

You knew *my child's* special needs long before the
doctor's words fell upon our ears.

No matter what life brings, *this child* is a gift from you,
and you know the details of every day of *my child's* life.
Please use *my child* to display your love and grace to me and
others.

Be honest with God. Tell him exactly how you feel. Share your disappointments, fears, and anger. Reveal any self-blame you are hiding in your heart. Today is the day to give all guilt over to God. Share with a friend. Write a letter. Visualize putting your guilt into a basket and handing it over to God. And don't take it back!

So how do we handle the disappointments that come our way? What happens when a church youth leader says, "Your child with special needs cannot attend our youth group?" How does a parent respond when the church turns its back on a child's special needs? Wendy's parents move from hurt and anger to a positive solution in the following story—"Noooooo!"

Noooooo!

WENDY'S MOM

Noooooo! I cried hysterically. This is the place where my child's supposed to be unquestionably accepted. She has to be allowed to attend!

The leader from the church junior high group had just informed me that Wendy, my thirteen-year old daughter, could not participate in the youth group due to her asthma.

"But she gives her own medication, uses her inhalator, and carries an emergency breathing treatment!" I retorted. "What-if my husband and I become parent sponsors?"

He didn't answer.

"What-if we train someone in case of an emergency? What-if I sit in the car in the parking lot, and no one knows I'm there?"

The leader sat there stone-faced, not saying a word.

Finally he sighed and replied, "No. We have no parent sponsors, and there is a liability of training someone for an emergency. I'm sorry."

The pain of not finding a support system at my church stung. It ran so deep that my husband and I thought we would never heal. Yet we believed the church leader truly thought he was looking out for the best interest of the church. We also believed that our church, as a whole, would not find the leader's solution acceptable. However, as Wendy's parents, we had no strength to fight this battle. We were crushed that our child had been referred to as a liability.

Privately we wrestled through our anger and disappointment. Then we brought the situation to God in prayer. We told him all about the leader who had hurt our daughter and had left us feeling betrayed by our own church. We then trusted God to restore our child and to give my husband and me the wisdom we needed to parent Wendy through this sad time in her life.

My husband and I felt devastated. Even though we were used to people feeling uncomfortable having Wendy around, the hurt did not sting less. We knew people were fearful of her condition because she landed in the hospital at least once a year. She had not been invited to several slumber parties for just this reason.

Wendy, on the other hand, hosted more slumber parties than a house should stand through. We planned each one carefully, as if we were planning an annual ball. The more parties Wendy had, the more Wendy's friends and their parents became comfortable with Wendy's unpredictable asthma.

God answered our prayers. In time we met exceptional people who, despite their concerns about Wendy's asthma, were willing to be informed and educated about Wendy's needs. Wendy recently was even invited to join the others and "slumber."

Regardless of their hurt feelings, Wendy's parents knew that God wanted them to forgive the church leader for his lack of understanding and unwillingness in helping to meet their child's needs. Despite their disappointment and anger, they were able to forgive. They realized that forgiveness is not an emotion or a response to emotion, but an act of obedience to God.

Wendy's father said, "Through this experience we have learned that forgiveness is the key to moving on. The leader at the church? Oh, he's still there and still in leadership. Do we think he truly understands the agony his decisions created for our family? No, we doubt it. Did he ever say he was sorry? We wish we could say he did. But regardless, we have forgiven him and have found a new church that isn't afraid of Wendy and her special needs."

Feeling accepted and being able to participate in social settings is crucial for everyone, including our kids with special needs. Yet this often isn't possible due to unfounded fear, lack of education, and simple unwillingness on the part of others. First Baptist Church in Redlands, California, realized this need, and the congregation acted on it.

"Kids come from thirty miles away to attend David's Corner, a Sunday school class we designed for children with special needs," Kimberly Hovey says. "David's Corner was built on the vision of a church member who lost her four-year-old son to complications from cerebral palsy. Her family had struggled with including him in their church life, because the average Sunday morning program does not have the staff or facilities to accommodate children with special needs. This mother dreamed of starting a Sunday school program specifically designed for any child with a special need, and her dreams became a reality. Six years later we continue to offer music, crafts, a Bible lesson, and a snack to a handful of children who attend. One family joined our church because they knew their son with autism would be well cared for while they enjoyed the church service. Some of the other parents of our students even attend other churches in town and use the hour as respite care, a time to worship as a couple.

"'David's Corner is one of the most important things we offer as a church,' my associate pastor reminds me. Perhaps what is important is that we are there, together, trying to make sense of God's love for all of us. When we need a reminder, we ask Brian, one of our students, 'Where does Jesus live?' and without missing a beat, he smiles and pats his heart. Brian has figured it out. For a child who might have been discarded as someone who cannot be a productive member of society, he knows the one thing that matters most of all: God loves us and seeks to dwell in our hearts. Sometimes that's all the understanding we need."

It is possible for many children with special needs to be mainstreamed into an existing Sunday school or youth program. Wendy was one of those students who, despite her special needs, could have participated in her youth program. Through our discussions with many parents of "special" kids, we've found that mainstreaming kids can be successful with the willingness of the church, with education, and with involvement from the parents. These parents also echoed one another in saying, "It's critical that families with children with special needs belong to a church that can meet the spiritual needs of all family members, and sometimes this requires change."

When issues and concerns arise, it's important to find a way for these special children to fit in. Janet found an excellent way to make sure her daughter, Jenna, was growing spiritually and making Christian friends. Janet shares Jenna's story in "My Treasures, My Friends."

My Treasures, My Friends

JANET LYNN MITCHELL

Junior high can be the toughest years of a gal's life. Not only had I lived through those years myself, but now I was reliving them with my daughter, Jenna. I watched as Jenna struggled to meet new friends and fit in at her new school. Like any teenage girl, hormonal changes raged. If that wasn't hard enough, Jenna began using an insulin pump to help control her diabetes. Life for Jenna had become complicated, and it left her feeling lonely.

"Mom, I'm always left out. There's another slumber party, and again I'm not invited," Jenna cried. "I understand that my friends from school are afraid of my diabetes, but Mom, even the girls at church are afraid of me!"

Again I found myself speechless. Jenna was right. Even though she was bubbly and could be the life of any party, she was often not invited due to her medical condition. Tonight was no different. I held my daughter as she cried herself to sleep.

The next morning I woke Jenna early. "Honey, I want you to get ready for school. I thought I'd take you out for breakfast so we can talk."

"Talk? Didn't we do enough of that last night?"

"We've got to quit feeling angry and left out. We need to do something about it!"

"What?" Jenna asked in a tone of *here she goes again*.

Within the hour Jenna and I sat waiting for our scrambled eggs and toast.

"Honey," I began, "last night I lay awake for most of the night. I had a great thought, and I want to run it by you. You know, there are several girls in our church who are not in a Bible study or active in the youth group. I think we should call and ask them if they would like to join a small group Bible study. I saw the movie *Troop Beverly Hills*, and I'd love to become the leader of ten girls."

That afternoon, as soon as Jenna ran in from school, she phoned the girls on our list. To Jenna's surprise, the girls and their mothers were excited about the idea.

Knowing how much fun and work this would be, I approached my cousin Megan. "We could lead this group together. You're in your twenties. You could surely bridge the generation gap!" I said, trying to recruit her.

Moments later Megan agreed.

Our first official meeting was a slumber party. By midnight ten girls who hadn't known each other were now laughing and carrying on as though they had known each other for years. We found that each girl struggled to fit in. Yet they didn't know why.

The girls and I organized. Friday nights would be our official meeting night, giving them all something to do on the weekend. The girls named our group the "Treasure Seekers" since we were seeking treasures in God's Word and in our friendships.

For the next four years the Treasure Seekers met on a regular basis. We worked on a weekly Bible study, "camped" in hotels, and learned about fashion and how to become women of God. The girls even designed rings and held a ceremony committing all that they were and ever would be to God.

When the Treasure Seekers began, Jenna and I had thought she was the one with special needs. What we found were ten girls from five different schools who appeared to fit in, yet all felt alone. The Treasure Seekers provided a place for Elise, struggling with dyslexia, to be accepted. We all supported Rebecca when she was diagnosed with scoliosis and began wearing her brace. We stood by Christina while her parents divorced. We prayed for Valerie and her family while her grandmother suffered with cancer. We cried with Danielle when her father died. We were speechless when Vanessa's grandmother was killed in a car accident yet cheered with the best when Vanessa was voted student body president of her high school. We stood in line for rides as Lindsay was the first of the bunch to get her driver's license. We kept Kate's secret. We laughed and celebrated with Laura when she was elected to the Homecoming Court of her high school. We provided love for one girl who was thinking of taking her life.

By creating a place for my daughter to fit in, I also provided a place for other girls to *belong*. And in doing so, I've had the privilege of loving ten girls, who have now become beautiful women. I truly did find a treasure!

Author and speaker William Arthur Ward says, "A true friend knows your weaknesses but shows you your strengths; feels your fears but fortifies your faith; sees your anxieties but frees your spirit; recognizes your disabilities but emphasizes your possibilities." These words describe the Treasure Seekers.

Friends are a gift from God. Proverbs 27:17 says: "Iron sharpens iron, and one man sharpens another."

Good friends challenge you to be your best. They remind you that you can when you insist you can't. They tell you that God even weaves mistakes into his plans.

At times, good friends may fail you, disappoint you, and forget to call. They may also cause you to grow when you would rather not. Janet says that they may even encourage you to forgive and celebrate by bringing you a "Balloon Bouquet."

The Balloon Bouquet
JANET LYNN MITCHELL

While in high school, I suddenly found myself bound to a wheelchair. The surgery to straighten my tibia, due to a birth defect, was—to say the least—unsuccessful. Within the next three years I spent more than 170 days in a hospital and underwent eight additional surgeries. From a body cast to the parallel bars and Forest Gump steel braces, I learned to walk again.

It was not until fifteen years later that one of my doctors confessed. The poor surgical outcome that I experienced was due to medical errors made during my first surgery. Little did my parents and I realize that the additional surgeries on my right leg were an attempt to correct the mistake. For fifteen years my parents and I were lied to by those we trusted with my medical care, and now my medical records and X-rays had been destroyed.

The initial shock of this news soon settled, and I was left with an anger that brewed. It was no surprise to me that on one of my gloomy days, my friend, Annette, paid me a visit. Annette is the most positive person I know. She can find the good in almost any bad situation. At that moment I couldn't find any good whatsoever in what had happened, and I wasn't ready to hear the good that Annette would ultimately find. *Sometimes there just might not be any good to find,* I thought.

Yet there Annette stood in my family room, holding a large balloon bouquet in an array of colors. Smiling from ear to ear, she eagerly announced, "Today is the day of forgiveness."

I laughed and wondered if she had accidentally inhaled a little too much helium. I reviewed my mental calendar. *Is it a Hallmark holiday I don't know about?*

"Listen, Janet. Today is the day you can forgive the doctors. It's time, you know. I've brought these balloons to help you forgive."

Now Annette had my attention. How in the world could this silly bouquet of balloons help me with the forgiving process?

With great persistence Annette proceeded to share her idea with me. She spoke words she knew I not only needed to hear but also needed to receive. "These balloons are for you to *let go.* We'll get a marker and write on them the people and situations you need to forgive. You know, the doctors and all. Then you can take a moment and choose to forgive."

The highlight of Annette's plan was that once this forgiving had taken place, we would proceed outside to a private place, and I would release the balloons to the heavens, setting them free! This would symbolically represent that I, too, had handed over my situation to God and *let go* of the pain and anger that held me bondage. This act would be a symbol marking my decision—the forgiveness that had taken place.

While listening to Annette and her idea, my stomach drew up into knots. I am not ready to set my balloons free! I'm not ready to say that what happened doesn't matter!

There had been a huge medical mix-up—a big blunder! Unsuccessfully blinking back my tears, I stood up and turned from Annette. With my fist clinched and lips quivering, I shamefully cried, "Don't you understand, Annette? I can't do this. I'm sorry, but I'm still too angry!"

Annette gave me a moment to catch my breath. She then stood, taking my hands into hers. "Janet, your forgiving will not change the past. It will just free your future."

What? She's crazy! I thought. *How can my act of forgiving release my anger?*

It took some work, but I proceeded to convince Annette that my forgiving needed to be a personal thing. Before saying good-bye, I promised her that when I was ready and when it was just "me and God," we would take care of things.

Secretly I knew that not one of my balloons would find its way to freedom in the skies that day. I quickly gathered their strings and hurried up the stairs, pulling the balloons behind me. I felt like a child trying to hide my unforgiveness, stuffing it way in the back of my closet, covering my balloons with my party clothes. That night as I lay in bed, I wondered if my good friend had picnicked on her porch, watching the sky for a sign of my healing progress.

More than three years passed after Annette blessed me with the balloon bouquet, and spring cleaning led me to my closet. It was while sorting and stacking, I found the balloon remains. While Annette had lived those past three years experiencing all God had for her, my soul resembled the balloons—weathered, shriveled, wasted away, and lifeless. Jolted by my discovery, I phoned Annette to tell her about the balloons.

Annette was positive my next breath needed to be words to my Heavenly Father, forgiving the men who had hurt me. "Janet, you don't have much choice. You will live the rest of your life with the consequences of someone else's mistakes and sin. The only choice you have is how you're going to live it."

Then I remembered what Norm Wright had told me: "Christ was able to forgive a wrongful death—his! He clearly understood the emotional distress and physical pain he was about to experience on the cross. Yet he forgave. Jesus forgave by speaking words! Jesus didn't wait to forgive until he felt like forgiving. He didn't wait until his pain had eased or reconciliation had occurred. No one had been punished. Christ's forgiveness did not depend upon the repentance of his enemies. It had everything to do with being obedient to his Father."

I sat speechless. I pictured Jesus on the cross, his body throbbing with pain from the piercing of each nail—and it was *then* that he forgave.

For the past three years Annette had understood something I did not. She knew forgiveness needed to begin with a decision to forgive. Annette taught me that forgiveness is a choice, not an emotion. Jesus taught me that it could be done!

Many of us have experienced hurt at the hands of others and are struggling with the issue of forgiveness. Whether the person was a doctor who made a mistake, a friend who just didn't understand your child's special needs, or perhaps a spouse who deserted the marriage vows—all because of an ability to cope—forgiveness is in your control.

Annette taught Janet that forgiveness is a choice, and Jesus taught her that it could be done. Annette did not force Janet to forgive. She respected Janet's need to grieve and be angry before she was able to forgive her doctors' concealment. Annette allowed Janet to forgive on her own terms, in her own timing, and in her own way.

Corrie ten Boom stated after her release from a German concentration camp that forgiveness is like a clanging bell. Long after the bell has stopped ringing, the vibrations can still be heard. Feelings of hurt and anger might linger long after the actual act of forgiveness.

Dave Stoop, a Christian psychologist, says that forgiveness does not always mean reconciliation. Janet chose to forgive her doctors, but she certainly did not return to them for treatment. After confronting them, wisdom dictated that she remove herself from any future contact with these physicians.

In her heart she fully forgave them and moved on with her life. Yet for a lifetime she will carry the scars of their mistake.

You can ask God to help you forgive those who have hurt you or your child. Do this in your own timing and in your own way. Forgiving may not mean forgetting, but it does mean moving forward with your life.

When God is about to do something great, He starts with a difficulty. When He is about to do something truly magnificent, He starts with an impossibility.
—ARMIN GESSWIN

Chapter 6
DEALING WITH THE IMPOSSIBLE

My Dreams Died and So Did My Faith
A MOTHER

When my daughter was born, my dreams of a healthy, *normal* child died—and so did my faith. Deep in my heart I struggled with anger, even anger toward God. Before my daughter's birth I had tried my best to live a life that would honor God. Yet when I truly needed him, I felt he abandoned me. My thoughts were so horrific, I couldn't share them with anyone.

So tell me, God, were you asleep during the formation of my baby? Have you turned a deaf ear to my cries? How could you desert me in my hour of need?

I felt empty. I had no tears left to shed. Shaking my fist and falling to my knees, I poured out my rage. I screamed and shouted my way through every bitter thought and emotion I felt—regardless of how atrocious they were. I was honest with God, and I told him how I truly felt. When I was through venting, I asked God to give me peace to make it through the next hour. For the first time in my life I experienced the peace of God spoken in Philippians 4:7: "And the peace of God, which surpasses every thought, will guard your hearts and your minds in Christ Jesus."

The remarkable peace this mom received once she poured out her heart to God came to her despite her circumstances and was not a result of positive thinking. This peace was God's gift to one who ultimately knew that he is in control.

God desires to hear our prayers. Like parents eagerly listening to their children's joys, struggles, and needs, we too have God's full attention when we pray.

"But my thoughts are so horrific that I could never share them. I can never tell God how I truly feel!" you may say.

Yes, you can. Nothing you'd ever say could shock God. In fact, the psalms are full of examples of people pouring out their true feelings to God. In these passages of Scripture, you can read of believers who cried out to God from their depths of despair, and you will also hear them singing to him in thankfulness. No matter what your feelings are, God desires that you share them with him.

These psalmists also recorded a number of accounts where God appeared to be silent. His presence was neither seen nor felt. Like the psalmists, you may feel God is silent in your life. You may not see his hand tending to your child's needs. You may long to feel his presence. These are the times you need to look beyond your feelings and meditate on what you know.

Another mother found that God is present, his character is unchanging, and his promises are true. She tells her story in "My Prayer Closet."

My Prayer Closet
A MOTHER

In the past when I didn't know what to do, or I had a problem, I went into my prayer closet. I dropped to my knees and bowed my head, and

God met me there. He provided an answer. Yet when my heart was breaking watching my child struggle each day, and I truly needed heavenly guidance, the God whom I loved seemed silent. I could no longer see or feel his presence.

Longing to feel his nearness, I clutched my Bible to my chest. Nightly I slept with it next to my heart, yet I found no relief. Confused, I didn't know what or how to pray. Exhausted, I found myself unable to pray. My communication with God turned into literal moans from the depth of my pain. In a sense I was in my prayer closet, refusing to leave.

My head told me to stay in my prayer closet and wait. My emotions said, "Why bother? God doesn't care what happens to you." My logic told me to put on the armor of God, wear it proudly, and stand firm!

My heart faintly cried, "I'm weak. I can't stand it any longer." When I reached this point, I curled up in my prayer closet and waited. That night I told God where I was. I stopped my frantic search for his presence during the silence. I left it up to God to find me.

As Scripture promises, God met me right where I was. He had not abandoned me. I now know that God had entrusted me with his silence. Despite what I had thought or felt, I know he heard my prayers.

Now I clearly understand what Reverend Rubin Welch meant when he eloquently stated, "With God, even when nothing is happening . . . something is happening." God's silence means that he's busy, working on my behalf, taking care of what concerns me!

King David also experienced the silence of God. He definitely thought God was slow in acting on his behalf. He reached a point of despair as he dealt with sickness, loss, and circumstances that overwhelmed him. David's words found in Psalm 13:1–2 reflect the depth of his pain: "Lord, how long will You continually forget me? How long will You hide Your face from me? How long will I store up anxious concerns within me, agony in my mind every day?"

God may appear to be silent in your situation too. You may not see his hand at work caring for your child's special needs. It has been said that "the greatest test of a Christian's life is to live with the silence of God." It's awesome to know that we can honor God by how we deal with the silent times.

Like David, we must trust God despite his silence and despite our circumstances. We must trust him through the waiting, the disappointments, and our darkest moments.

During a difficult time Janet discovered that God promised to be with her through it all. She shares her story "In the Dead of Night."

In the Dead of Night

JANET LYNN MITCHELL

The piercing sound of Joel's apnea monitor sounded in the dead of night. In my semiconscious state, I flew out of the extra bed in Joel's room in which I "slept" each night. With adrenaline flowing, I rushed to grab my young son, prepared to perform CPR. Hearing my yell for help, Jenna, age seven, joined me, turning on the lights in the room.

To our amazement, there was baby Joel, happy as could be, holding his unplugged lead that attached to the monitor, thus causing the alarm. Joel had learned a new game. Whenever he wanted something, he could now get immediate attention by merely pulling the lead, thus sounding an alarm!

After calming down my entire family and putting everyone back in their respective beds, I finally lay down again. I could hear the steady beat of my own heart. From the corner of my eye, I observed Joel's chest movements in perfect rhythm with his breathing. *Another false alarm.* I sighed as I closed my eyes, trying to distract myself from the concerns of my young child.

Not being able to sleep, I leaned over and reached for my "flip book," a book in which I had written special Scripture passages and affirmations. "Another night with no sleep," I moaned. I was certain this lack of sleep was detrimental to my disposition, not to mention further complicating the depression that I fought.

With one hand on the book and the other holding a flashlight, I nestled down under my covers, prepared to read. Through the fading beam of my flashlight, I read words by Granger Westberg in his book *Good Grief*: "Depression is not something unique just to you or me; it is an experience that seems to come to all people when something they love and treasure dearly is taken away from them."[1]

My next entry read: "Even strong men like David cried out when they felt depressed and alone, as shown in Psalm 5:1–3: 'Listen to my words, LORD; consider my sighing. Pay attention to the sound of my cry, my King and my God, for I pray to You. At daybreak, LORD, You hear my voice; at daybreak I plead my case to You and watch expectantly.'"

I read those words over and over. I needed to be reminded that I was normal, but if I'm normal, can someone tell me why I'm lying wide awake when I desperately need to be sleeping? If I'm normal, why then am I sneaking like a child to read and fill my mind with facts of hope?

As hard as I tried to lift my spirits, my thoughts and emotions failed me. I knew that I had a lot to be thankful for. Yet my emotions knew no logic. Depression overwhelmed me, sleep was unpredictable, fear of the future surprised me at awkward times, and tears flowed freely. I even wondered if I was a disappointment to God since I couldn't seem to conquer the blues.

Over time my childhood faith and belief system had been shattered. I had always believed that because I was God's child, he would protect me and my young family—that he was an invisible shield that separated me from anything that could ultimately hurt me or my children.

Yet I realized my belief system was wrong. Through Scripture I learned that God had not promised to be my insurance policy, but he had promised to be with me through the trials and unfortunate circumstances in my life. Isaiah 43:2–3 says: "When you pass through the waters, I will be with you; and when you pass through the rivers, they will not sweep over you. When you walk through the fire, you will not be burned; the flames will not set you ablaze. For I am the LORD, your God, the Holy One of Israel, your Savior" (NIV).

Looking back to that night and the following months, I now smile. I see what I couldn't grasp then. God faithfully walked by my side through the rivers, through the fire, through the depression—through it all!

Janet made it through that difficult time in her life. She fought depression, shed tears over what could have been, and waited for God to strengthen her. She trusted God as she prayed and filled her mind with

Scripture. Janet held to the promise of Psalm 3:3: "But You, LORD, are a shield around me, [You are] my glory, and the One who lifts up my head."

Jeanne Pallos writes:

But what about the times you don't feel God's presence? What about the times you cannot read your Bible or pray, and your trust in God seems exhausted? What do you do when you feel your life sinking into a deep chasm?

As Christians, we often think our feelings of anger, fear, depression, and despair are wrong. God gave us our feelings. They are like warning lights on the panel of a car that tell us when our lives are on overload or something is seriously wrong. Don't ignore the warning lights in your life.

Here are Jeanne's suggestions for what to do with your feelings when they seem to overwhelm you.

- Be honest about what you are feeling. It's OK to say, "I'm feeling angry. This seems so unfair." Write about it, talk about it, and pray about it.
- Join a support group for parents of children with special needs.
- Seek professional counseling for needs the support group doesn't meet.
- Have someone you can call anytime—day or night—and who will listen to you. This might be a therapist, someone from your support group, or a trusted friend.
- Try to get enough sleep. This probably sounds impossible, but sleep when the child/children sleep. Housework can wait. Sleep deprivation can lead to depression, illness, and despair.
- If you are feeling suicidal or afraid you might harm your child, seek professional help. Share these feelings with your support group or pastor. Contact a local suicide prevention hotline or a child abuse prevention center. These agencies are listed in the front of your phone book, and the services are free.
- Seek medical help if your feelings of despair and depression keep you from functioning or sleeping. Our bodies are affected by our feelings and circumstances, and many times chemical imbalances occur in the brain. When talking, praying, and resting don't resolve the depression, talk to your doctor.

- Ask God to guide and lead you to places where your heart can find encouragement, strength, comfort, and healing.

Chapter 3 of Daniel tells the story of Shadrach, Meshach, and Abednego. In spite of their circumstances, they chose to honor God. When they were brought before King Nebuchadnezzar, he said, "Now when you hear the sound of . . . music, if you are ready to fall down and worship the image I made, very good. But if you do worship it, you will be thrown immediately into a blazing furnace" (v. 15 NIV).

Shadrach, Meshach, and Abednego did not waiver in their faith, nor did they allow the pressures surrounding them to result in compromise. Boldly they answered King Nebuchadnezzar: "If we are thrown into the blazing furnace, the God we serve is able to save us from it, and he will rescue us from your hand, O king. But even if he does not, we want you to know, O king, that we will not serve your gods or worship the image of gold you have set up" (v. 17–18 NIV).

These three men trusted God to deliver them and were determined to remain faithful regardless of the consequences. Shadrach, Meshach, and Abednego were thrown into the blazing furnace, but God sent a heavenly visitor to accompany them through the flames in their time of trial. These three men experienced God's protection and weren't harmed by the intense flames. Their example of faith demonstrates how God can be trusted even when we can't see the future or predict the outcome.

Kay Raugust shares the faith of Shadrach, Meshach, and Abednego. She learned how to trust God in spite of her trials. Kay shares her story in "I Wuv You."

I Wuv You

KAY RAUGUST

When I became pregnant at the age of forty-three and a routine amniocentesis revealed Down syndrome, I realized my life as I knew it was over. Yet I never imagined that this would include my marriage.

My son, Michael, was a fighter from the beginning. At birth he was diagnosed with eleven medical problems, including Down syndrome, an enlarged heart, blood poisoning, leukemia, and anemia. He also had the lowest white-blood-cell count with survival that the hospital had ever experienced.

For his first three months Michael's development paralleled his siblings, Jim and Susan, but then he began having seizures, resulting in a hearing loss. By the time he was nine months old, he was totally deaf. Jim, Susan, and I began to learn sign language so we could find ways to communicate with him.

Just when I thought we were beginning to manage Michael's special needs, I found myself at the end of my rope. Michael developed reflux and began throwing up many times a day. My clothes, my furniture, and even my carpets experienced the results of Michael's upset tummy. "God," I cried, "I can deal with several of Michael's disabilities, but not the reflux!"

A few weeks later my kids and I ventured out to an evening service at church. As I stood chatting with friends, Michael threw up carrots all over my shoulder and down my new polyester dress, leaving a permanent stain.

Once home, I put in a load of wash. As I poured soap over the clothes, I asked God for a sign. "Lord," I prayed, "if you're going to heal Michael, please show me by removing the carrot stain." When the cycle ended, I pulled the dress out of the washer. As I held it up, tears filled my eyes—the stain was still there.

"Lord, I know that was a silly prayer." Determined this was not going to shake my faith, I clutched the dress to my heart and cried, "You know, God, I'm going to trust you in spite of the stain!" Then I threw the clothes in the dryer.

To my amazement, when I removed the dress from the dryer, the stain had vanished! Two weeks later Michael was seizure free while on medication, and his reflux was gone. God had answered my prayers, and each day he gave me the endurance to take care of Michael's special needs.

Soon after, God was still answering my prayers. When Michael was almost a year old, another special thing occurred during a shopping trip with my mother. Seeing a sale item I wanted to buy, I stepped into a store and left her in the mall with Michael in the stroller. When I returned, she said excitedly, "Michael spoke! He said, 'I love you.'"

I was certain my mother had imagined Michael's precious words until later that evening when Michael looked up at me with a smile and said, "I wuv you." My heart skipped a beat.

A few days later Michael returned to physical therapy. The therapist was sitting on the floor with Michael leaning against her. While she talked to me, Michael watched her closely. He turned his head, trying to look behind his back, and even tried to turn his head upside down while smiling at her. "I wuv you," he said quietly.

Without thinking, she replied, "I love you, too, Michael!"

Excitedly I shouted, "Wait! Wait! Didn't he just tell you he loved you?"

"I guess he did!" she said in amazement. He must have regained part of his hearing.

My life totally changed the moment Michael was born. As Michael's mother, I can honestly say that I've cried more, prayed more, and hoped more than I ever had before. I can also say that I have loved more than I ever knew possible. Yes, God gave me the gift of three precious words, and now I daily repeat them back to him. "I love you!"

Kay's outlet and joy is working in the handicapped ministry of First Evangelical Free Church of Fullerton, California. This church offers three special-needs Sunday school classes for children and one for adults. Through this ministry Kay found a way to give back to the people and the community who have been so dedicated to her son.

Kay said, "My first job at the church was putting crafts together for the typical children. When I discovered that Michael was coming home with crafts from the classes I worked with, I offered to develop lesson plans and crafts for the kids with special needs. I developed a year's worth of lessons. I color Bible picture stories in advance for the two classes of severely handicapped kids, but I leave things out so they can add items to the pictures and feel they participate in creating them. And best of all, Michael absolutely loves Sunday school!"

Mary Magdalene and Mary, the mother of James, loved Jesus. They, like Kay, faced a monumental problem that they did not let stop them. The Sabbath had ended, and these women, accompanied by others, were on their way to the tomb to anoint Jesus' body. They talked as they walked along the road. Mark 16:3 records part of their conversation: "Who will roll away the stone from the entrance to the tomb for us?" they asked each other. Despite the fact that these women knew they could not move the stone themselves, and they had no idea if anyone would be there to move the stone for them, they kept walking toward the tomb. They expected a miracle—to get past the guards and reach their Lord. Once there the women saw the stone rolled back and an angel sitting on it! God blessed the actions, devotion, and determination of these women. They were the first to witness the resurrection of Jesus!

Deb Haggerty and her husband, Roy, wanted to help Roy's son, Jimmy. They also faced obstacles and were unsure how their "stone" would be rolled away. Yet they knew their Heavenly Father would see that it was done. Deb shares her story in "Oh, I Get It!"

Oh, I Get It!

DEB HAGGERTY

"Hello," I said as I answered the phone.

"Deb, it's Diane," the voice on the line announced. "Is Roy there?"

I handed my husband the phone, then grabbed my coffee, and sat down. The caller was my husband's ex-wife.

"Roy, they want to hold Jimmy back a year," Diane told Roy. "His teacher says he's not ready for first grade. I don't understand. Jimmy loves school and wants to learn how to read."

Roy stood silently holding the phone. "Diane, you know that I'd love to help our son. I'm just not sure how I can, living so far away."

The conversation soon ended. With no solutions in sight on how to help my stepson, Jimmy, Roy and I began to pray.

A few days later, while I was playing bridge with friends, I related Jimmy's woes.

"He sounds just like Kyle!" my friend Nancy exclaimed. "Maybe Jimmy learns differently too."

"What did you do about Kyle?" I asked, eager to find a solution.

"We took him to Dr. Gold. He's a great doctor, who is wonderful at getting to the heart of the problem with kids who learn differently."

That night I shared Nancy's story with Roy. He was excited about the possibilities and called Diane. "Diane, why don't you send Jimmy here for a visit so we can have him tested by Dr. Gold."

A few days later we were standing at the airport eagerly waiting to greet Jimmy. We had a wonderful night together, and the next day we headed into New York City to meet Dr. Gold. Several hours passed before we heard the verdict. Jimmy did have learning problems. He both saw and heard things differently from most kids.

As Jimmy slept in the backseat on the way home, we agonized over a solution to the problem. Dr. Gold's recommendation was for Jimmy to work with a learning consultant and an occupational therapist. How was Diane, who worked full-time, going to handle taking Jimmy to appointments several days a week?

After many long distance calls and much discussion, Diane made a very heroic, self-sacrificing choice. "Roy, you and Deb have the ability to care for Jimmy and the training nearby he needs. I don't. Why doesn't Jimmy live with you during the school year, and I can see him summers and school vacations?"

With that decision, a wonderful, blonde-headed, eager little six-year-old came to live with Roy and me. Many days of investigation later, we found the perfect specialists to work with Jimmy and also found a Montessori school.

Jimmy kept telling us, "I'm going to learn to read! I'm going to learn to read!" But at first he didn't.

After months of little progress, all of us were frustrated—Jimmy most of all. We prayed that a breakthrough would occur, but as time limped by, the chances seemed slim. Then one spring day a teacher from the school excitedly called us. "I think I found the solution! I was watching Jimmy work a maze. He studied it for a long time and then drew it perfectly. If I can show him the end results and how the letters fit together to get there, I think we can teach him to read."

Working with flower petals of consonants around a center of base words, she showed Jimmy how language worked. "See, Jimmy? This petal 'B' and the center of the flower 'at' spells *bat*. Add the petal 'C,' and the center spells *cat*."

Jimmy's eyes lit up. "Oh, I get it! I get it! Then this is *mat*, and this is *rat*, and this is *sat*."

"Right, Jimmy."

"Then this is *man* and *can* and *ran* and *tan*." The breakthrough we'd prayed for had occurred. Jimmy was on his way.

Lots of time and patience, a perceptive doctor, a creative teacher, a self-sacrificing mom, a dad who wouldn't give up, a boy who wanted to learn, and me (a stepmom open to God's plans) all worked together to allow God to help this special child bloom.

When Roy and Deb heard of Jimmy's problems, they prayed. They asked God to direct them as to how they could best help Jimmy. They knew that obstacles such as distance and custody were not problems for God. They held onto Jesus' promise in Matthew 17:20: "For I assure you: If you have faith the size of a mustard seed, you will tell this mountain, 'Move from here to there,' and it will move. Nothing will be impossible for you."

Deb and Roy's story is a true example of God working—touching the hearts of *all* parents involved. It's a story of one parent releasing her child when she never thought she could bear being separated from him, and two parents making room in their lives for a blonde-haired boy.

Parenting kids with special needs requires parents to go the extra mile—to do things they never dreamed of doing and to teach lessons that only parents can teach. Tyler Sexton, a teenager living with cerebral palsy, tells his story of a great lesson learned in "Thank You, Sweet Potato."

Thank You, Sweet Potato

TYLER SEXTON

Although I was right there in the midst of all the controversy and chaos that surrounded my premature birth and subsequent life-and-death struggle to survive, I obviously don't remember any of it. What I do remember, from my earliest childhood on, is my mom's beautiful face being the last thing I would see before going into one of my many surgeries and the first thing I would see when I awoke. Is it any wonder that I love her so deeply?

Of course, I love my father and sister every bit as much as I love my mom, but the relationship between Mom and me is, well, special. I don't remember where or when I came up with the nickname "Sweet Potato" for her, but anyone who knows her will admit that it's a perfect fit.

I remember one of the few times when I started to feel sorry for myself. I was in the fourth grade, and I had been out on the playground at school, trying to do jumping jacks with the rest of the kids. That day we had a substitute PE teacher who was unaware of my condition. When he saw my clumsy attempts at exercise, he thought I was clowning around, so he hollered out in front of everyone, "What's wrong with you, kid? You're in the fourth grade, and that's the best you can do?"

I felt humiliated. I couldn't wait to get home and hide in my room. When Mom came in to check on me, I told her about my day. "I'm tired of being me," I cried. "I'm tired of having cerebral palsy. I don't want to do this anymore!"

I could tell from the look on her face that her heart was breaking, but instead of pitying me, she stood up and went straight to my closet and started taking all my personal things—toys, games, *everything*— and tossing them out of my room.

"What are you doing?" I demanded. "Stop!" But she ignored me and continued tossing until there was nothing left for her to throw away.

It was awful. Angry tears poured down my face, and I felt so betrayed. Why would the one person I felt closest to and trusted above everyone else do such a terrible thing? Finally she stopped. She came over and sat down next to me on the edge of my bed.

"Do you know why I took everything from you?" she asked, looking me in the eyes.

I shook my head no, but I didn't say a word.

"Because I can," she answered. Then she waited a minute, giving me time to think before she continued. "What *can't* I take from you, Tyler?"

"I don't know. I don't know," I answered, sobbing between words. "You already took everything."

"No, I didn't," she said, catching me off-guard. "I didn't take the person God made you to be. Tyler, no one can take that unless we let them. People can break into our home and rob us, taking everything we have, but no one can steal who we are, because God made us. He made you, Tyler, and you're a blessing to everyone who knows you. And that's all that really matters."

I've never forgotten the lesson my mom taught me that day. I may have a physically limiting condition, but that condition doesn't define who I am. God is the only one who has the right to do that. And since he wrote the Scripture that says I'm fearfully and wonderfully made, then I guess it must be true.

Thank you, Sweet Potato, for having the strength and wisdom to teach me that great truth.

---

1. Granger E. Westberg, *Good Grief* (Minneapolis: Fortress Press, 35th Addition, 1997), 31.

Jenna, Joel, and Jason Mitchell

Mikayla Steele

Laura Shepherd

Brooke and Paige Dunning

*Jenna Mitchell with her
mom Janet*

Matt Payne

Bryson Tuttle

Laura Shepherd with her mom Linda

Karlson Ruhle

The Treasure Seekers

Susan Tacklind

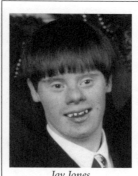

Jay Jones

Robbie, Elizabeth, and Michael Paddock

Rick Osborn

Jason Mitchell

Robbie Kosman

Eric Winter

Lauren Briggs and Marita Littauer

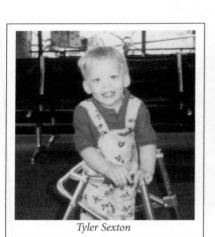

Tyler Sexton

Keith Jay

Genna Stanford

Trent Burris

Steven and Daniel Osborn

Sabrina Coleman

Brook Ellenson

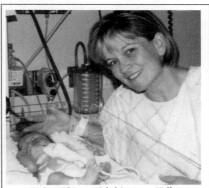

Brian Clauss with his mom Kelly

Jonathan Drennen

Caitlin and Jonathan Pulone

Taylor Osborn

Timmy and Nathan Addison

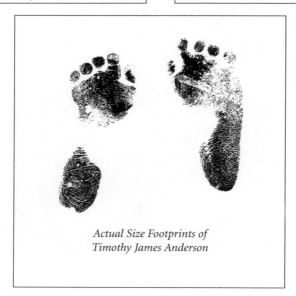

*Actual Size Footprints of
Timothy James Anderson*

Courage is fear that has said its prayers.
—BITS AND PIECES

Chapter 7

DEVELOPING COURAGE THAT COUNTS

Courage in Spite of . . .

AMY'S MOTHER

"If you want to talk, just let me know," the nurse said before closing the door.

Want to talk? I screamed silently. *I don't want to talk about it! I won't talk about it. No one will ever know.*

I walked over and stood by the hospital crib where my baby lay sleeping. With one hand I smoothed the blanket that covered her, and with the other I adjusted one of the many tubes entering her tiny body. My eyes stung as I stared at the monitor that flashed with every beat of her heart.

Why now? Why did it have to happen while my husband is halfway around the world trying to save his business? How can I tell him such news when he's so far away? What will I tell my family and friends?

I paced the floor. How would my church respond if they ever found out? God, why can't you show the scientists a cure? Why does AIDS have to be a death sentence?

Wiping my tears, I walked back to the rocking chair and sat down. Slowly I began to rock, hoping to rock myself to sleep. Instead, random thoughts filled my mind. My precious Amy was barely six months old. She had been only three days old when she was placed in my arms. The adoption wasn't even final. Yet she was mine. She was my baby, and I was her mommy. Then today, when I was bursting with motherly pride and joy, I suddenly found myself crumbling with sorrow.

"God," I prayed, "I don't think I've ever felt this alone, this scared, this overwhelmed. There's a constant lump in my throat, and my heart throbs with pain. My friends call, and I sit unmoved, watching the telephone while it rings. I'm falling apart, God! I don't sleep. I don't eat. I feel myself pulling away from those who love me. I just want to be left alone. This is my secret to hold forever!"

The door to Amy's hospital room opened. "Can you tell it's me?" my girlfriend asked, giggling behind her required mask, gown, and gloves. "Gayle, how are things today?"

Today things are terrible! I wanted to shout. Instead I said a silent prayer, asking God to give me the courage to confide in my dear friend.

"Gayle," Kathy repeated. Her eyes then penetrated mine as though she saw straight through me. In a second, her arms were wrapped around me, and I was held secure in her love.

"God," I begged again, "please give me the courage to confide in a friend."

Gayle found the courage she needed to confide in her friend, Kathy. It didn't happen right away, but weeks later, after Kathy had consistently stopped in to check on Gayle and had phoned her often. Kathy showed that she genuinely cared about Gayle and her family, and she earned Gayle's trust. Kathy was one in a million!

What would have happened if Gayle had chosen to remain silent about her daughter's medical condition? Unfortunately, many parents of children with special needs make this choice. From not knowing what to say or how much to say, to simply not wanting to talk about it, parents all too often keep their concerns to themselves.

Scripture tells the story of David and his loyal friend, Jonathan: "And Jonathan made a covenant with David because he loved him as himself" (1 Sam. 18:3 NIV). When King Saul was trying to kill David, Jonathan warned him a number of times at the risk of his own life. Then in 1 Samuel 20:42, Jonathan said to David, "Go in peace, for we have sworn friendship with each other in the name of the LORD, saying, 'The LORD is witness between you and me, and between your descendants and my descendants forever'" (NIV).

David honored his covenant with Jonathan many years later when King David discovered that one of Jonathan's sons, Mephibosheth, was still alive. At five years of age, Mephibosheth had become crippled in both feet when his nurse fled with him after hearing about the death of Saul and Jonathan.

King David summoned Mephibosheth and told him, "Don't be afraid . . . for I will surely show you kindness for the sake of your father Jonathan. I will restore to you all the land that belonged to your grandfather Saul, and you will always eat at my table" (2 Sam. 9:7 NIV).

As you read these passages of Scripture, you will note that the years of David and Jonathan's relationship were filled with outside conflicts. Yet their bond of friendship was one in a million. So you ask, "What happens if I can't find that one-in-a-million friendship? What-if the friends who once stood by my side have returned to their jobs, kids' sports, and social activities?"

One mom said, "When my child was first diagnosed, my husband and I were surrounded by family and friends. Yet now, almost a year later, although my child is still fighting cancer, my phone has quit ringing. It's true. My life has drastically changed in the past year. I'm no longer a room mom in my child's class at school. I no longer attend PTA meetings, Bible study, or church. It's not that I wanted to quit these activities, but I just can't go—I can't leave my sick child! I sometimes wonder if my friends, who once stood by my side, have forgotten about the cancer treatments. They have moved on with their own lives as I sit at home alone and count each day as precious."

Patricia Paddock, too, found her life drastically different once Robbie, her child with special needs, was born. She says, "I felt isolated, like a prisoner in my own home, because Robbie's fragile health made it almost impossible to take him anywhere. I was not experiencing all the imagined joys of being a mother—no MOPS meetings or play days at the park. Every time I saw a healthy baby, I wanted to cry."

Patricia, like Gayle, learned a valuable lesson. They both now can say, "A friend is someone who knows the song in your heart and can sing it back to you when you've forgotten the words."

Author and speaker Len Wein says, "A friend is someone who is there for you when he'd rather be anywhere else."[1] Patricia Paddock needed this kind of a friend. She tells her story in "A Special Place for Special Moms."

A Special Place for Special Moms
PATRICIA PADDOCK

My son, Robbie, was born with multiple disabilities. He has cerebral palsy, is blind and developmentally delayed, and has a seizure disorder. The first two years of his life, it was hard to go anywhere due to his fragile health. I was essentially homebound with him.

From age two to three, he attended a therapy center, which had a support group for the moms while their children were in therapy. After the previous two years of isolation, I found it wonderful to be around other moms of children with special needs. Unfortunately, the center only provided services for children through the age of three.

When Robbie turned three, I felt sad. I knew that I needed an avenue for fellowship with other moms so we could share our life experiences, support one another, and share in our joys and sorrows. I knew if I went to MOPS (Mothers of Preschoolers) the focus would be on issues of parenting typical toddlers and preschoolers. I knew I would be brought to tears because I would never know typical parenting experiences with my child. I needed friends who were going through what I was going though. And I needed friends who would be by my side through my child's preschool years to adulthood.

I began to dream of a place where special moms could gather and love one another's special kids. My dream became a reality when my church stepped alongside of me, offering me a room in which to meet, a coffeepot, and child care for the siblings of kids with special needs. I made flyers announcing the first meeting of the Special Moms/Special Kids group, and the rest is history.

The Special Moms/Special Kids group has given moms a place to celebrate the impossible as our children achieve each milestone. One day we celebrated as one mom realized that her child's fussy time was normal. This mom is now going home to enjoy those fussy hours, knowing that her baby is doing something typical.

Our meetings don't have much of an agenda. That takes care of itself as we use our time together to talk about the relevant—our current challenges, concerns, and triumphs. Occasionally we have a special speaker, or we make a craft. Yet most of our meetings consist of sitting around a table, munching on goodies, and sharing our experiences.

Through Special Moms/Special Kids I have found a lifeline of emotional support. Sometimes just being in the presence of another special mom lets me know I am understood and am not alone in this journey. How blessed I am that I followed my heart and found the courage to seek out other moms, moms who needed me just as much as I needed them. How blessed I am!

It's been said, "The best part of our journey of loving children with special needs is the people we meet along way."

Lee Ann met Jeanne in the story "Courage to Share" (chap. 3) when Lee Ann moved into a new neighborhood. Wanting her neighbors to become aware of her special needs child, Lee Ann sent letters to them introducing her son, Timmy. Jeanne was a neighbor who received one of those letters and befriended Lee Ann.

Since that time Lee Ann has given birth to another "special" child, and Jeanne has continued to be Lee Ann's friend. As Jeanne says, "I've offered her 'My Hands' and my willing heart!"

My Hands

JEANNE GETZ PALLOS

My neighbor, Lee Ann, became pregnant with her second child and developed complications in the sixth month. Nathan was born three months early and was not expected to live.

For Lee Ann and her husband, life became a balancing act, juggling their time between Timmy, their child with autism, and Nathan, still in the neonatal intensive care unit.

I wondered how I could help but then decided that Lee Ann and Jim probably didn't need people bothering them at such a stressful time. Plus, they had family nearby, so I stayed away. Yet I couldn't get the thought of this family in crisis out of my mind.

"I just don't know how to help them," I said to another friend with "special" kids. "What can I do?"

"Talk to them," she replied. "Ask them what you can do to help."

After Nathan came home from the hospital, I sent Lee Ann an e-mail: "I've been thinking about you and wondering if I can help you?"

To my amazement, Lee Ann wrote back and asked if I'd like to wash Nathan's bottles?

"Of course," I wrote back. "I'll come by today."

Washing bottles took less than half an hour. "Lee Ann," I said, "this seems so small. Isn't there something else I can do?"

"If you didn't wash these bottles," she said, "I'd be up after 10:00 each night washing them. This is a huge help!"

Each day as I washed the bottles and syringes, I prayed, "Lord, use the nourishment that flows through these bottles to bring healing to this child."

One evening when I returned the clean bottles, Lee Ann invited me in. "Can you stay and talk for a while?" she asked. "Jim's at school." I settled on the sofa and kept her company as she gently fed Nathan.

Timmy, her six-year-old, woke from his sleep. "Can you hold Nathan while I check on Timmy?"

Holding out my arms, I caressed the precious baby.

After Timmy was settled, she returned. "Lee Ann," I said, still holding Nathan, "I've been afraid to help you care for Nathan, and I don't know how to relate to Timmy. I've never been around a child with autism. Will you teach me?"

"Of course," she said. "I'd love to. I wish more people would ask."

Walking home, I smiled and thought, *I am able to help my friend, Lee Ann. I've offered her my hands and my willing heart.*

Jeanne wanted to help her friend, so she took it upon herself to ask what she could do. So often fear and lack of knowledge keep people from reaching out to families with children with special needs. Jeanne offers some suggestions for you to help a family in your church, school, or neighborhood.

- Ask the family what they need.
- Organize a group of people who can bring in meals, help with cleaning, do laundry, and go shopping.
- Offer to take older children to their activities. Include siblings in car pools, even if their parent is unable to participate.
- Call when you are going shopping and find out if there is something the family needs.
- Offer to go along to doctors' appointments.
- Make sure you and others are not sick when helping the family!
- Encourage the couple to spend time together. Offer to babysit or take the children to your house for a sleepover.
- For a housebound couple, create a romantic evening by bringing in a special meal. Set their table with china and candles. Arrange for someone to watch the children for a few hours.
- If the family in need is in a location unfamiliar to them when a crisis occurs, contact a church in the area and ask if someone can minister to the family.
- Be resourceful by helping the family find services they need.
- Be available for emergencies. Offer them your work and/or cell phone number.
- Be a friend. Listen, care, and pray—offer your two hands and a willing heart.

It takes courage for parents of children with special needs to ask for help. Many times they assume their need is obvious. As Jeanne stated in her story "My Hands," she knew her friend Lee Ann was in crisis, yet she had no idea how to help. Through communication Jeanne discovered that Lee Ann had needs that could be met by Jeanne's own two hands.

Candy Burris, too, found she had a need—a need that, if known, could have been met by a church. She tells her story of being far away from home and family, living in a new town. In spite of it all, Candy found "A Reason to Be Courageous."

A Reason to Be Courageous
CANDY BURRIS

I used to think that courage was a trait a person was given at birth, sort of like inheriting a mother's blue eyes, a father's height, or a grandfather's stubborn personality. Over the past several years, I have come to realize that courage resides in each of us. It will rise up at times when we least expect it, usually during crisis moments.

Shortly after the birth of our fourth child, Trent, we were thrust into a world that was totally unfamiliar to us: a world of hospitals, doctors, and laboratory technicians. Trent, we were told, had multiple abnormalities. He was born with three holes in his heart, a heart valve that wasn't functioning normally, and an enlarged liver. His blood test results were high in areas that should have been low and low in areas that should have been high.

Heart surgery was imminent. The doctors scratched their heads, trying to provide an adequate diagnosis on an infant who was failing quickly. The pieces to the complicated puzzle were not coming together, and our family seemed to be falling apart. Having recently moved to Grand Rapids, Michigan, we were in unfamiliar territory. Our church, our support group, and the vast majority of our family all resided in Ohio.

We were alone, scared, and totally unprepared to handle the crisis that confronted us. Dave and I took turns staying with Trent at the hospital. With three other children at home, one of us would stay the night with Trent while the other would make a meager attempt at normalcy on the home front. In the morning the one at home would load the children into the car, drive the thirty minutes to the hospital, and spend ten minutes exchanging updates while the kids peered through the small window of the NICU unit to view their brother.

On occasion the nurses would allow the older kids to enter the room so they could stroke their brother's dark hair or hold his tiny hand. The parent who spent the night at the hospital would then load the kids back into the car and head for home to catch up on a few hours of precious sleep before making the swap again after lunch. It was a vicious cycle that left us physically and emotionally drained.

One morning, after a particularly rough night, I drove home, grabbed my camera and about five rolls of film, and quickly returned to the hospital. I spent the day taking pictures of Trent. I was so scared that he wasn't going to make it that I wanted something to remember him by.

It has been said that when you reach the bottom, you finally get smart enough to realize you have to look up. I applied this to my life. Independent by nature, I usually prided myself in being able to handle most crises that came my way. However, this was life and death, and there was nothing I could do within my power to change the situation.

I realized early on that Trent was a gift from God. Whether I had that gift for three years or thirty was not up to me. He was in the hands of our Heavenly Father. Realizing this was a turning point for me. I no longer battled the "what-ifs." Although I knew the grief would be more than I could bear, I realized I would not have to handle it alone. God knew what he was doing, and I had to trust him.

Trent made it through his first year and continued to battle the odds. When I look back over the past years, I can see definite areas of growth within our family and myself. We have learned to trust God, not just when a crisis arises but in our day-to-day journeys. Our faith has been strengthened, and we feel blessed beyond measure to have Trent in our lives. Trent has taught us to face our fears. He has taught us to live each day as if it could be our last and to make a difference now. Trent has taught us to look beyond our own little worlds to find areas where we can impact others. Most importantly, he's given us a reason to be courageous.

Candy said it, and we believe it. The children with special needs whom we love have given us all a reason to be courageous!

Sometimes this courage is seen when we say that we can, even though our emotions tell us we can't. Sometimes this courage is found in our words when our children ask "Why?" or "Will this hurt?" And sometimes this courage is seen as we do what we know is best for our child despite how we dread it. Sabrina's mother experienced this first-hand when she placed Sabrina on a bus headed for "A Camp for Good Times."

A Camp for Good Times
JO COLEMAN

One of the hardest things I've ever had to do was to put my daughter, Sabrina, on the bus headed for Camp Ronald McDonald for Good Times, a camp just for children with cancer. Sabrina was eight years old, and it had only been a week since she had her left leg amputated. But despite my fears and her apprehension, off she went as I bit my lip and watched my bald-headed daughter apprehensively wave through the window.

Sabrina suffered from Ewing Sarcoma, a rare form of bone cancer. At the time only five hundred pediatric cases were known in the U.S. For the past year we had ridden a roller coaster through three courses of chemotherapy—only to conclude with amputation.

"But Mom, I've never been to camp," Sabrina had stated with concern.

"If you get lonely or it's too much, we'll find a way to bring you home," I assured her. "But we think you'll have fun and will enjoy getting away from the hospital for a while."

Now, years later, Sabrina looks back and shares her feelings regarding this camp experience: "It was really hard, especially at first. After being with my mother and grandmother 24-7, it was hard to be without them. With a new amputation my sense of balance was off. I was still trying to get comfortable using crutches and wondered if I'd ever get the hang of it. I wore a cast on my stump and therefore couldn't swim with the rest of the kids. I couldn't even take a shower, so I had to take sponge baths. Also, I experienced phantom pains—pains that were real in a leg that wasn't. But the hardest thing of all was being around other children who didn't have appendages missing. I was the only amputee! Even though everyone had cancer and was nice to me, I felt like an oddball."

In spite of the obstacles that faced her, Sabrina stayed at camp until the last day—when she was driven straight to the hospital. Her white-blood-cell count was so low it was cause for concern. With lumps in our throats, my husband, Charlie, and I met her there.

At the hospital we found our daughter beaming and covered with dirt from head toe. "Mom, I had a blast at camp! Can I go again next year?"

Hearing Sabrina's words, my husband and I were convinced that our decision to send her to camp was the right one.

Within moments Sabrina's favorite nurse, Marta, entered the room. "Hey, girl, I hear you've been to camp. The first thing we've got to do is clean you up!" Marta proceeded to undress Sabrina and help her bathe. She then helped the doctor as he removed the cast off her stump.

"What's this?" Marta exclaimed while taking a step backwards. "Just how many crickets did you bring home?"

I looked over and saw the dead cricket now lying on the examining table next to Sabrina. I thought for sure I would pass out. Sabrina still had staples in her wound, and I was certain that awful bug carried a million germs. Sabrina was again placed in isolation, and we had to suit up to visit her because of the danger of infection. Her immune system was destroyed due to chemotherapy.

When Sabrina was first at camp, she cried almost every day, "I'm never going again." Yet once home, she told doctors, nurses, and anyone who would listen to her, "I had a blast at camp! I want to go again next year!" And back she went every summer after that. Sabrina has met many kids over the years, all suffering from some type of cancer, all fighting to live. She counseled the first-time amputees and comforted them.

Sabrina has continued to help others deal with cancer and its often devastating outcome. She is currently planning a conference for young amputees to encourage them and help them network together.

Sabrina said, "The first time I saw anyone with an amputation was when I was seven. I went to a waterslide, and the girl working at the top, punching the cards and telling which slides you could go down, had lost her arm. I wondered why she had lost it, and when someone said, 'She lost it going down the slide,' it scared me. Not knowing 'why' is hard. To ask is normal.

"So whenever people look at me wondering, particularly little kids, I always stop to answer their questions. I want them to understand that I can do anything I want to do. I'm fine even though I had cancer.

"I am completely content with what has happened in my life. Some small things are a constant reminder of having cancer—of having a prosthesis. Things have been tough but not too bad. I have learned to respect life more and to respect God for always being here for me," Sabrina said in conclusion.

As Sabrina's mother, I know that God was with us as we walked the journey through Sabrina's cancer. I know that he gave me the courage to put Sabrina on the bus and send her to Camp Ronald McDonald for Good Times, a camp where she met other kids with cancer and just had fun.

∞

It's hard to imagine the courage Sabrina and her parents displayed as they exchanged their last hug just before Sabrina was wheeled off for surgery—to remove her leg. This courage was something they never knew they had until the instant it was needed. As he did for Sabrina and her family, God will provide courage to you and your child at the moment you need it most.

In a letter written by Corrie ten Boom in 1974, Corrie wrote about a time during the Nazi invasion of Holland when she faced fear and wondered where her needed courage would come from.

When I was a little girl, I went to my father and said, "Daddy, I am afraid that I will never be strong enough to be a martyr for Jesus Christ."

"Tell me," said Father. "When you take a train trip to Amsterdam, when do I give you the money for the ticket? Three weeks before?"

"No, Daddy, you give me the money for the ticket just before we get on the train."

"That is right," my father said, "and so it is with God's strength. Our Father in Heaven knows when you will need the strength to be a martyr for Jesus Christ. He will supply all you need—just in time."

Yes, loving kids with special needs takes courage—courage given to us from God that teaches not only life's lessons but teaches our children how to live with their handicap and/or manage their disease. Yes, it takes a courage that says, "Let your child try and fail. Let him spread his wings and learn to fly!"

Janet shares a moment of courage in her story "She's Eighteen."

She's Eighteen

JANET LYNN MITCHELL

I leaned over her bed and brushed Jenna's hair away from her eyes. This was not the way she should be spending her eighteenth birthday. But despite our hopes of a wonderful party, my daughter was confined to a hospital bed and hooked up to an IV.

As Jenna slept, I watched her intently, pondering the past twelve years. *Silly me.* I somehow thought that when Jenna grew up, life would be easier. I must have been dreaming to think that with age she would gladly assume the responsibilities that go along with her special needs. Now I know: *Life's just a different kind of hard.*

At eighteen, Jenna, a senior in high school, wants to fit right in like any other teen. Yet she finds it nearly impossible to plan beyond today. She's a moment-by-moment type of gal. Unfortunately, her carefree spirit causes her to forget to test her blood, give herself insulin, and chart the results. She thinks she's invincible. Yet I know better.

Today, as I watch her sleep, I wonder what her future will hold. I wonder if life will ever become easier for her and if she will ever totally conform to having juvenile diabetes. I stop myself short of thinking of the horrific consequences that diabetes can bring.

"I'm now eighteen," Jenna announced with confidence. "I can take care of myself!"

"Sure," I said, remembering our conversation.

"But, Mom, you've got to let go of me. You've got to let me try!"

Immediately I felt a lump forming in my throat. For the past eighteen years, my job had been to take care of my daughter. And now on a day's notice, Jenna wanted to fire me from the job!

I sat quietly and prayed, "Lord, please help Jenna to put into practice what I taught her the past several years. For today is the day I knew I would someday face. It's a day that despite my motherly instincts of wanting to mother her, I need to step back and entrust Jenna fully to you. Yes, today is the day I say, 'From my hands to yours.'"

---

1. Len Wein, *The American Bathroom Book* (Lan C. England, Compact Classic, 1992), 3-C-2.

One of the greatest and most comforting truths is that when
one door closes, another opens; but often we look so long
and regretfully upon the closed door that we do not see
the one that has opened for us.
—NUGGETS

Chapter 8

OVERCOMING SETBACKS AND STANDSTILLS

A Date in the Shade
DANIEL'S FATHER

"It's been a year since we've gone on a date," I said to my wife.

With no solution in sight and not wanting to stir the pot of anger that simmered, my wife pretended she had not heard me.

"It's been a year. . . ," I repeated as my wife broke into tears.

Again, I said the wrong thing, or maybe the right thing at the wrong time. But there was *no right time* to talk about the circumstances that overwhelmed us. Our son, Daniel, had been born premature and suffered from multiple handicaps. Daniel's needs were met daily. It was my wife's and my needs that were sacrificed and overlooked. It was obvious to us—we needed a date!

Child care was a problem. My wife and I didn't know anyone who was willing or felt comfortable to babysit. Ironically, we understood our friends' and family's fears and feelings of inadequacy in caring for our child. We, too, had felt them the moment we brought our son home from the hospital—and we lived with them daily. This, however, didn't change the fact that my wife and I desperately needed time away together.

I'll never forget the afternoon when my wife's mom knocked on our door with a picnic basket packed full. "I've come to send you and Becky on a picnic this afternoon. I've even brought this special blanket for you to picnic on."

How can we picnic? I thought sadly. *We can't even leave the house together!*

Before I knew it, Becky's mom was in the house watching our son, and we were spread out on the special blanket picnicking under the large maple tree in our own backyard. What a gift of love! Becky's mom gave us what we truly needed—time to be alone and time to spend with each other. Although we never left the property lines of our home, our date in the shade was a gift that Becky's mom could give since she was comfortable watching our child if we were just a holler away.

It's true. Becky and I needed time to be together, time together without one eye on our baby's heart monitor, time to laugh like school kids under a tree. Unfortunately, not all parents of kids with special needs have parents as insightful as Becky's mom. Yet we all can learn from her example and share it with our friends who genuinely ask, "Is there something that I can do to help?" If so, some of you may find yourselves sleeping under the stars and actually camping in your own backyard while your friend or family member tends to your child "just a holler away."

Many of us understand the dilemma Daniel's parents faced. We know one of the most difficult things to deal with is that our children's needs are never ending. It takes courage to ask for help and to let others know our needs. What we must remember is that God did not intend for us to walk this journey alone. If we do not communicate our needs and express our concerns to our friends, our needs may go unmet.

In Mark 2:1–12, Mark tells the story about a paralytic man and his four friends. These four saw the needs of their paralytic friend and wanted to bring him to Jesus. Conquering any obstacles they may have faced, they carried the paralytic man to the home where Jesus was preaching. Once there, because of the enormous crowds, they couldn't get near the door. This, however, did not stop these friends from completing their mission. They picked the paralytic up, mat and all, and carried him up the stairway that led to the roof. Determined to bring their friend to Jesus, they dug a hole in the mud-and-straw roof and lowered him down to the feet of the Son of God.

Jesus' reaction is given in verse 5: "Seeing their faith, Jesus told the paralytic, 'Son, your sins are forgiven.'" And in verse 11, "I tell you: get up, pick up your stretcher, and go home." This lesson teaches that we must never underestimate how the faith and love of our friends can impact our lives.

Charles shares a story of how he and his wife, Jennifer, were blessed by a friend on a mission in "A Life-Changing Visit."

A Life-Changing Visit
TIMMY'S DAD

Even though we knew help was available, for some reason I felt it was Jenny's and my responsibility to fully care for our severely handicapped child. We had not taken advantage of the services that could have made our lives easier as well as benefiting Timmy. While I worked two jobs, trying to make ends meet, the bills mounted on my desk. My wife's life revolved around a child who could neither move nor communicate.

Jenny's social life was nonexistent, and she found little reason even to get dressed for the day. I often arrived home from my night shift to find Jenny curled up in the overstuffed chair adjacent to our child's hospital bed, located in the family room where she "slept" at night. Jenny truly loved Timmy, and so did I, yet we were physically and emotionally exhausted. We had forgotten what it felt like to sleep through the night. We had even forgotten what it felt like to laugh.

One morning we heard a knock at the door just as I was grabbing my jacket to leave for work. I went to the door as Jenny rushed for her robe. Within minutes we found ourselves sitting in the family room. Our pastor stood over Timmy's bed and looked past the tubing and sounds.

"Timmy, it's good to see you again," he said. Continuing on, Pastor John got straight to his point. "Timmy, I've met some people who would love to come and get to know you. In fact, they would like to stay with you a few mornings or afternoons a week so that your mom and dad could run a few errands or attend a Sunday service. Maybe they could even go out for dinner. I am sure that once you get to know these people, you'll want your parents to go out weekly. I'm told Maggie, one of these nurses, knows great jokes."

Finishing his conversation with Timmy, Pastor John walked over to where we were sitting. Too tired to argue with him, I let him talk. He said, "Charles, I've found out that you can receive financial help for meeting Timmy's needs through Social Security. Once you apply and Timmy is accepted, you can quit your night job. After a long day Jenny deserves to have you home with her. And you two deserve to go on a date!"

Along with this news Pastor John told me of the many women who had expressed an interest in bringing lunch and coming by to visit Jenny. They were just waiting for the word to get started. At last Jenny had a reason to get dressed.

It's been two years since Pastor John made that *bold,* life-changing visit. Timmy now receives a monthly check from Social Security (SSI). I now work one job, and we attend church weekly. Timmy's awareness of those around him has improved some, and he even grins at Maggie's jokes.

Little did I know two years ago that God never intended Jenny and me to bear the burden of our son's condition by ourselves. It seemed the harder we tried, the more impossible it became to manage without help. How grateful I am that I did not forsake the wise counsel of our pastor and that I allowed angels in disguise to come into my home a few times a week and love our son. Yes, how grateful I am.

Charles and Jenny felt overwhelmed while caring for the needs of their son, Timmy. They not only needed some time to themselves and time to spend with each other, but they also were in desperate need of a good night's sleep. Sleep is critical for our mental and physical health, and the constant depletion of it lowers one's ability to cope, adds to depression, and can even alter one's judgment.

One mom said, "The best thing you can do for your children is to get enough rest so you can be at your best!" How true it is that many of us who are caring for children with special needs do not always get the sleep that is required. Unexpected circumstances arise, adding to our already existing responsibilities of managing a home, tending to our child's health needs, and maintaining employment. Sleep, therefore, becomes a last priority.

Janet remembers a night when *exhaustion* could not begin to describe how she and her husband felt. They had both just crawled back into bed after rushing to respond to what turned out to be a false alarm blaring from Joel's apnea monitor. As they settled down, they watched the glow from Joel's monitor—the red light flashing with every beat of their son's heart.

"Janet," Marty whispered while he lay facing Janet's back.

"Whatcha need?"

"I need you to turn toward me so we can talk."

"Marty, I'm so tired I can't move. Just talk loud so I can hear you."

Upon hearing how silly this sounded, Marty started laughing. Janet joined him and laughed until there were tears in her eyes. Looking back, the Mitchells learned that even though their hearts ached and they were drained, it was possible to find humor and to convulse with laughter.

"Humor eases the sting of pain and makes life livable," Marty said. "Laughter is a holy gift from God."

Janet and Marty did laugh their way through those difficult years. They also made a conscious effort to keep their marriage alive and healthy. "I found a copy of our marriage vows and framed them, placing them on the mantle in our bedroom," Janet said. "Daily we were reminded of our love and the commitment we made to each other. Marty and I had promised to be each other's best friend, and best friends we would work to be!"

Karen Kosman and her husband did not share Marty and Janet's experience. Despite Karen's desire to have her husband by her side while dealing with their son's special needs, Karen's husband retreated, and there was no laughter. They experienced a "Marriage in Trouble."

Marriage in Trouble

KAREN KOSMAN

My husband couldn't seem to accept that our son, Robbie, had a learning disabililty and a speech impediment. Privately, we'd argue. Difficulties grew at home as angry words became a common practice and frustrations mounted.

"Karen, he's lazy, and you're too easy on him," Ted shouted.

"Why don't you spend more time with your son instead of yelling at him all the time," I spouted back.

"Because he never listens to what I tell him!"

"Ted, you're not a failure because your son has special problems."

I thought, *Why do I feel alone in all the stressful, serious situations that arise? We have a son whose needs are so great. Yet I receive only silence and rejection from Ted. What's wrong with his heart? Why does he treat Robbie like he's a mistake? Why can't Ted and I work together to help our son?*

The more I read about learning disablties, the more I understood why Robbie struggled so. I also learned that the emotional tug-of-war Ted and I were having was typical of some families of children with special needs.

"Lord, help us to be a loving family," I prayed.

These types of questions are not only asked by Karen but by thousands of parents of children with special needs—trying to hold together the pieces of their marriages. Marriage and parenting are tough enough without adding the mixture of mounting medical bills, fatigue, emotional strain, social challenges, and grief. Adding to these challenges is the fact that couples often deal with grief as individuals. Therefore, one spouse may be in a completely different stage of the grieving process from the other.

One thing is for sure. Couples who face the challenges of raising a child with special needs will either grow closer through the experience or be torn apart. They will rarely remain unchanged. All too often, parents of children with special needs become strangers living under one roof. Yet marriages can survive and thrive if nutured with time, commitment, faithfulness, and love.

There are times, however, when despite the prayers, marriages end. Jennifer Jackson shares her story in "My Mummy-Daddy!"

My Mummy-Daddy!

JENNIFER JACKSON

One look and we both knew! The tiniest seventeen-month-old baby we had ever seen was destined to be our daughter. It was a spiritual moment, a moment of deep understanding, of looking beyond the present to something not yet realized. No explanation was necessary. Our eyes met as Ray held her, and we knew.

A remarkable series of events saw us take our adopted daughter, Crystal Maria, to our home at Canyon Creek on the Alaskan Highway. Then began the long journey toward understanding how her little fetal alcohol syndrome (FAS) mind worked, and it was usually opposite to what was expected!

We were immersed in the joys and challenges of family life for several years. Each indication Crystal learned something new was cause for great excitement. We were so proud of her and freely shared her latest achievement with everyone. Yet we saw the shocked glances, the hesitation, and the curious looks followed by a step back—especially when she did not perform the latest accomplishment being discussed. Her blank gaze with half-closed eyes caused people to wonder about us. We overheard a lot of comments but looked beyond it all. We were a family, and we loved our little girl more than anything the world could offer.

Crystal always wanted her daddy. I often felt as though I was just there to provide her daily needs and keep her safe. Her love was reserved for Daddy.

Since we had learned children with FAS rarely bond with parents, I was thrilled when she wrapped her tiny hand around my finger one day while going for a drive to Otter Falls on the Aishihik Road.

"Ray," I whispered, "she's holding my finger!"

We were both delighted but shared the moment in silence, afraid the slightest sound or movement would release her grip.

Those happy, secure years passed quickly. Gradually the foundation of our marriage eroded away until the daddy Crystal lived to see and the husband I adored was gone. The happy days became a haunting memory, replacing joy with pain.

I trudged through the motions of daily life and watched as Crystal filled her emptiness with gospel music. At five years old she was tiny and fragile looking. Music became her life.

I interpreted her tiny sounds as she came to me and whispered, "Tape over," many times each day. Then she would go back near the tape recorder to enjoy another song, swaying to the rhythm as she became lost in the music.

After nearly two years of "living in a fog," Crystal brought me back to reality with a profound statement that revealed how deeply she was thinking. Sitting on my lap, she suddenly turned and smiled at me. "You my 'mummy-daddy'!" she announced decidedly.

"Well," I answered slowly, "I *am* your mummy."

"No!" she stated emphatically, pointing and tapping me firmly with her tiny finger as she spoke, "You my 'mummy-daddy'!"

"Yes, honey, I guess I am," I reassured her after a moment's thought. An expression of contentment crossed her little face as she hugged me, planting a kiss solidly on my cheek.

I said a prayer for God's help, watching in disbelief as she walked away, clutching an ever-present toy. Crystal had just allowed me the full responsibility for her life, and I felt the burden of it settle on me.

Crystal was becoming secure in our situation at last. She had never spoken like that before, and there was an unusual depth to her thinking. It seemed she now realized her beloved daddy was not coming home. Yet a little girl needs two parents. What she told me made sense, and with God's help, I would be her "mummy-daddy."

In Jennifer's story, her precious daughter, Crystal, came to realize the absence of her father. Crystal knew that she needed a mommy and a daddy, thus allowing her mommy to fulfill both roles. What Crystal does not yet understand is that she has a Father who cares for her immensely. Psalm 68:5 tells us that God is "a father of the fatherless." This means Crystal is covered by God's protection and provision. Jennifer, too, will be cared for by her Heavenly Father, as she truly is Crystal's "mummy-daddy."

Life with a child with special needs can bring difficulties, disappointment, and discouragement. Often the circumstances that occur are totally beyond our control. Yet no matter how tired we become, we don't dare quit. When brought to a standstill, we need to persevere and stand strong in the Lord.

One of the greatest examples of overcoming setbacks and standstills is found in the Old Testament. Nehemiah faced scorn, slander, threats, conflict, fear, discouragement, and unbelievable odds as he motivated the Jews to rebuild the walls and gates of Jerusalem. He conquered each obstacle with prayer, followed by action. When opposition arose, he did not pray, "God, get me out of this situation." But instead, Nehemiah prayed, "Now strengthen my hands" (Neh. 6:9 NIV).

Nehemiah showed tremendous determination and faith to remain committed to his responsibility. He did not focus on the troubles around him, but looked beyond them. He found people who rallied to his cause and worked by his side. The walls and gates of Jerusalem were rebuilt!

We, too, can echo Nehemiah's prayer, asking God to strengthen our hands as we care for our children with special needs. We can also rally the troops, seeking others to join us in accomplishing our task.

Susan shares her story of how she was able to join the ranks in helping her granddaughter accomplish a mighty task in "Reading Made Easy."

Reading Made Easy
SUSAN TITUS OSBORN

"Grandma, I feel sad," eight-year-old Taylor said as she plopped down on the couch next to me.

"What's wrong, sweetie?" I asked, placing my arm around her shoulder. I could tell that something was really bothering her.

"Well, it happened yesterday. I was sitting at the lunch table with a bunch of kids. We were all eating and talking about a movie we want to see. When all at once, one of the boys looked at me and said, 'How come you don't know those words we read today? Huh?'

"Oh, Grandma, I wanted to run and hide, but before I could do anything, another boy said, 'Yea, too bad you don't know how to read.'

Grandma, I didn't know what to say. I don't know why I don't know some of the words," Taylor said as her big blue eyes filled with tears.

My heart went out to my granddaughter, and I hugged her tightly. Then I looked at her with determination and announced, "I'll help you learn those words, Taylor. We'll read together, and then the boys won't have a reason to tease you anymore."

Within weeks of this conversation, the school resource specialist tested Taylor's second grade class. The test revealed Taylor had a learning disability. She could read individual words, but she had trouble putting them together in sentences and comprehending the meaning. Taylor began attending the resource center at school. There she received extra help in reading and language arts, and her reading improved greatly.

I, too, began encouraging Taylor. Whenever the grandkids came over, we'd spend time reading easy readers. I would read a page, and Taylor would read a page. If she stumbled over a word, I would help her without making a big deal of it. Then as six-year-old Shelby, Taylor's younger sister, began to read, the three of us would take turns. While we read, three-year-old Kolton sat patiently and listened to our stories. By taking turns reading in the relaxed surroundings of my home, Taylor became comfortable reading out loud.

As well as reading published books, I introduced them to the easy readers I was currently writing. My three young grandchildren soon became my editors. After we'd read the rough draft of one of my children's books, they offered suggestions for changes. One time I wrote, "The monkey reached for the rope."

"Grandma, the monkey grabbed the rope," Taylor said. "*Reached for* is boring."

And she was right—*reached for* is boring.

By taking the focus off how to read and placing it on helping me to improve my stories, Taylor felt important.

My next project was a picture book titled *Ten Friends Together*. After finishing it, I handed it to Taylor for her approval. She gave me a thumbs-up and asked, "When can I have a copy?" When she realized that the book wouldn't come out for another year, she suggested, "Let's make our own copy for Kolton for Christmas!"

And make a copy we did. I typed the words in a big font, dividing it like it would be in the published picture book. Taylor drew the pictures, one on each page to go with the words. And she did an out-standing job. Art is one of her best subjects.

"Taylor, you are a wonderful artist," I praised. "And you know, sweetie, if you have to struggle with a subject in school, I'm glad it's reading."

She looked surprised. "Why, Grandma? Reading's hard."

"Yes, it is now, but reading gets easier as you go along. You're good at math, and it gets harder every year. But every year reading will become easier and easier."

"You think so, Grandma? I can hardly wait."

Just as Susan helped her granddaughter learn to read, we all want to help our kids with the issues that concern them. Yet despite our wishful thinking, there are times when our efforts do not bear fruit and our attempts to help are just that—attempts.

So we try again, finding different ways and methods. For we know that we've truly only failed when we quit trying.

Linda Shepherd Evans shares a time when she tried and tried and tried again in her story, "A Big Birthday Cry."

The Big Birthday Cry
LINDA EVANS SHEPHERD

Have you ever wondered what it would be like not to be able to communicate? Although nine-year-old Laura cannot talk, she often communicates through a series of tongue and face signals. Plus, she can nod her head by chewing. Her smiles and frowns help her to communicate to her world. For example, through her signals, she recently let her tutor know that she could count up to nine—a skill we didn't know she possessed.

After hearing the good news, I gave Laura a hug. "Boy, Laura, you are one smart kid!" I said.

Laura frowned and stuck out her tongue in her pointed "no" signal!

"Yes, you are!" I said. "I understand you cannot always tell us what you are thinking, but that doesn't mean you are not smart. You are very smart."

Laura responded by showing me her "happy tongue," which she wagged down her chin.

Several days later, at her little brother's surprise birthday party, Laura was the most excited child in the room. All smiles, she couldn't wait to surprise Jimmy!

During the party she was thrilled to get a sack of party favors. With alert eyes, she watched a former circus clown juggle red balls before making silver quarters disappear into thin air. When the clown twisted a yellow balloon into the shape of a dog and handed it to her, she laughed silently. She was happier still when the clown painted a pink heart on her cheek.

While the other kids ate birthday cake, Laura licked icing off her spoon. Her eyes sparkled as she tasted her cold vanilla ice cream.

Finally, Laura grew tired and closed her eyes to tell her nurse she was ready to go back to her bedroom.

Later, as she lay in her bed, she began to sob. I went to her room to try to understand what had upset her. "Did something bad happen to you at the birthday party?" I asked.

Tears filled Laura's eyes as she gave me her "yes" tongue signal.

"Did someone upset you?" I asked, stroking her dark, silky hair. When Laura closed her eyes, I knew I was not on the right track.

"Are you upset because you did not get a birthday present?" I asked, desperate to make sense of her tears.

Finally, I got a nod!

I ran to my secret Christmas-gift stash and pulled out a videotape I had planned to give her on Christmas morning. I hurried back to her room. "Here's a present for you!" I told her, hoping to brighten her mood.

Still Laura grieved.

As I looked at her red face and puffy eyes, I wanted to cry too. I just couldn't understand what it was she was trying so hard to tell me.

Exhausted, Laura cried herself to sleep that night. I felt exhausted too. If only I could understand why she was so unhappy.

The next day Laura was no better. When I mentioned the situation to my friend, Mickie, she asked, "Did Laura get her party favor bag?"

"You know, I don't think she did," I replied thoughtfully. I marched back to Laura's room. "Laura, are you sad because you didn't get your bag full of birthday surprises?"

A grin spread across Laura's face! She gave me her "yes" tongue signal and nodded. I ran to the kitchen, found her bag, and brought it to her.

As we opened it, she cooed with glee. I pulled out a miniature plastic dinosaur egg and held it for her to see. When I opened it, Laura grinned as a plastic baby dinosaur landed on her chest. She smiled as I fastened a pink imitation watch onto her arm. I couldn't help but smile too. I was glad I had finally communicated with my daughter. Yet I was sorry it had taken me so long to do so.

Someday when Laura and I are in heaven, I won't have to read her mind. She will have her own words to share with me. But until that day, I'll do my best to be Laura's voice as well as her interpreter. But one thing is clear: Today Laura and I have no trouble understanding our love for one another. And for now that is enough.

A sense of humor can help you overlook the unattractive,
tolerate the unpleasant, cope with the unexpected,
and smile through the unbearable.
—MOSHE WALDOKS

Chapter 9
ACCEPTING THE FACTS

A Dream Come True
JANET LYNN MITCHELL

Every girl deserves parents as loving and determined as mine. At sixteen I lost the use of my legs. Even after several failed surgical attempts to correct the problem, my parents continued to reach for the stars—doing whatever it took for me to be permanently out of a wheelchair and walking.

"You simply need to accept Janet's situation and adapt her life around it," we had been told by doctors. Yet with X-rays in hand, my father and I boarded an airplane in hopes that an orthopedic specialist across the nation might think differently. The sound of the plane's engines revving up matched my father's determination to find me help.

Would this doctor in Georgia know something the doctors in California didn't? Or would I return home knowing that our dreams of finding help were just that—dreams.

Once there we met this famous orthopedic surgeon. With a striped dress shirt, a clashing bow tie, and a signature roadrunner belt buckle, he greeted us as if he had known us his entire life.

Surgery was performed. I awoke to find myself in a cast that began at my waist and ended at my right toe! As I recovered, my father stayed in a hotel a few miles away. Often he walked to the hospital to visit me—saving the pocket change of a taxi. He ate out of vending machine and whatever I had left on my food tray.

After two additional surgeries by the hand of this expert and several return trips to Georgia for physical therapy, my dream did come true. I conquered what seemed to be impossible. I rose from my wheelchair, faced the parallel bars, and met my challenge—walking!

Janet's parents gave their all and didn't give up hope of Janet walking again.

"Had the renowned surgeon in Georgia repeated the same diagnosis as Janet's previous doctors, we would have concentrated on helping her accept and adapt to life in a wheelchair," Janet's father said. "I'm glad that we reached for the stars. Janet's life has been brighter because we did."

How do parents of children with special needs know when to reach for the stars or know when they've done all they can to change their child's situation? They research, seek medical opinions, and pray for guidance. But the reality is, there will be times when all efforts to find help fail, and acceptance becomes a necessity. Yet this acceptance can be accompanied by determination and a drive to keep informed of the latest medical breakthroughs and scientific studies.

A terrific prayer to turn to during these difficult times is the "Serenity Prayer."

> God grant me the serenity to accept the things I cannot
>   change,
> The courage to change the things I can,
> And the wisdom to know the difference.

Julian's mother struggled with accepting the diagnosis her daughter had been given. She shares a time in her life when all was dark in her story, "Seeing with Her Hands and Heart."

Seeing with Her Hands and Heart

JULIAN'S MOTHER

I was in shock when the doctors sat me down and began to list the physical problems my infant daughter demonstrated. I felt devastated. I could hardly catch my breath. The dreams for my child's future and how I pictured motherhood had in a flash been shaken to the core.

A week later I numbly walked into the support group I had been *instructed* to attend. As a newcomer I felt vulnerable, too vulnerable even to look into the eyes of the other mothers. It was too soon for me to understand fully how these moms had survived.

As I headed for a seat in the back of the room, one brave mother took me in her arms. She recognized my pain since her ten-year-old son had the same diagnosis as my Julian. "I know the shock of discovering that your child is blind," she said. "But trust me, your tears will dry. You won't cry when you someday see what your daughter *can* do."

"But her world is dark. She is *blind!*" I said with tears streaming down my cheeks.

"Mary, I know that Julian can't see your face, but she can hear your voice, feel your touch, and smell your presence. Take her little hands and bring them to your face when you talk to her. You can teach her that there's a world around her. You can give her a reason to discover and learn. If she's not aware of her environment, she won't have the desire to communicate. Your daughter will learn to see despite her darkness."

"Do you promise this will happen?" I asked the stranger who seemed to know more about my child than I did.

"I promise," she said with a smile as she used her index finger to lift my head. Our eyes met. "Your child will see. She'll see, using her hands and her heart."

"Your tears will dry" were the reassuring words from a mom who had been there. To Mary these words seemed nearly impossible. Yet they were words she would cling to on her way to acceptance.

In time, Mary, too, began to see. Through the love, knowledge, and encouragement she received from her support group, she learned that her voice and scent would assure her daughter, Julian, of her presence. She learned that blind children do laugh, play, and even sing!

Support groups have proven valuable for many families. The energy it takes to participate is often returned twofold. Families who've attended support groups have verified that they no longer feel alone.

Carrie experienced a time in her life when she was surrounded by the love of her family and friends. Through their support and her deep trust in God, Carrie learned to accept the things she cannot change. Carrie's captures these memories in "A Moment in Time."

A Moment in Time

CARRIE PULONE

Just before Jonathan's first birthday, I realized I had few snapshots of my son and no professionally done photographs. Yet the walls of my home were canvassed with photos of my three-year-old daughter, Caitlin. Perhaps the reason was the emotional drain the past year had taken on us.

Jonathan had a degenerative genetic disorder. Doctors had warned that his time on earth would be short. There would be no first time Jonathan held his head up. There would be no first time he sat up alone or any first steps to celebrate. Yet this realization of not having pictures overwhelmed me with guilt. So I decided to take Jonathan down to the portrait studio where I always had my daughter photographed.

I walked into the studio filled with little ones ready to be captured on film. A lump formed in my throat as I heard children squeal with delight when the photographer jumped from behind the camera and shouted, "Peekaboo."

"That's a great smile," he praised one little girl.

Oh, how I wish this could be my experience, I thought with a sigh.

When it was our turn, the photographer brought us to a room fortunately out of view from all the onlookers. "Go ahead and sit him up on the platform," he said.

Immediately I wanted to say, *Sir, if you only knew how I prayed for that exact miracle each and every day.* But instead, I kindly replied, "Jonathan is unable to sit unassisted."

"OK, we have a chair he can sit in."

I began to feel as if I were the only mother crazy enough to bring her child with special needs to a photo studio for typical children. I took a deep breath then explained that my son would need support like that of a newborn.

"Can we get him to smile?" the photographer asked.

I stared back and shrugged my shoulders. In the ten-minute session allotted to my son, the photographer attempted to get him to sit up straight, smile, or even look toward the camera. All the while my stomach turned into twisted knots. This half-effort attempt resulted in a series of proofs that brought me to tears.

Determined to find a finished product that even somewhat resembled the beautiful, precious little boy I knew and loved, I tried two more studios. More tears. More disappointment.

By the time this horrific day ended, the only comfort I could find was taking my baby in my arms and holding him tightly. When it was only he and I alone together, none of the other things in life mattered. It's in these moments I realized that he is God's perfect child, and God chose to send him to me.

The challenges of many days came and went. Then one day a friend of mine invited me to a support group she had started. The group was called Mothers with Faith, a gathering of women who had children with special needs. At the first meeting I attended, the guest speaker was a photographer for a local newspaper who had a son born prematurely. She gave tips on how to photograph a child in the NICU. She said, "When taking a picture, get close up, as close as you possibly can. Use high-speed film and, if possible, natural light for a softer look."

She turned off the lights and gave a slide presentation that included photographs of her son. This was what I had been looking for, pictures of my son that looked like hers. *I can do this!* I thought. *I can learn to photograph Jonathan myself.* And so I did.

My husband purchased a camera and lots of film, black-and-white included. I discovered that while I wasn't able to get him to sit up, smile, or even look my way, I was able to capture the spirit of my little boy. I captured his precious profile—the same expression I loved to look at in the dark each night before he fell asleep. I captured his big bright eyes—the same eyes that made me melt each time our eyes connected for even the slightest moment.

I began experimenting with different backgrounds, different lighting, and different poses until the end products captured the spirit and the inner being of the little boy I knew and loved. I photographed Jonathan and Caitlin, capturing their relationship in a moment in time.

No more tears. No more disappointments in an unsuccessful photo shoot. Instead, my walls now hold priceless pictures I will treasure forever.

Carrie's pictures of her son are now priceless. Her precious Jonathan passed away nearly three years ago. Carrie says, "Every time I look at any of the pictures I took of him, I remember how beautiful his life was. I remember specific moments we had together. I remember what a true gift he was, and he will be part of my life forever."

Janet also feels that her children are a gift from God. Yet there was a time when she struggled with balancing their needs and hers until one day at thirty thousand feet she discovered how to perform "A Balancing Act."

A Balancing Act
JANET LYNN MITCHELL

When Joel was born premature and Jenna was diagnosed with diabetes, my life as I knew it vanished. I began to ride a roller coaster that was fast and furious. Regardless of my dreams, I had to accept the fact that until my children were grown and stable, my life would constantly be in motion. My children would always have needs, and at the drop of a hat, I would have to put down what I was doing and help. Their lives depended on it!

I chuckled to myself, remembering how I thought life was challenging before I had two "special" children. Yet after Joel was born, I was forced to juggle the needs of two children with health concerns, my typical son, my husband, and believe it or not, me!

It seemed I was the one whose time ran short. I put my children's needs first. Then I worked hard at meeting Marty's needs, even keeping a tidy home. Yet my needs, which could only be met by me, were often overlooked.

Who was I kidding? Everyone around me could see the frayed mother who hadn't taken time for herself. My life and appearance reflected what I truly believed—my needs belonged last on the priority list. I mentally sighed, *There is no time for me!*

It wasn't until I was on an airplane that it hit me as I sat pondering the instructions the flight attendant gave: "In the event that oxygen is needed, oxygen masks will fall from the cabinet above. Quickly pull the strap over your head and place the cup portion of the mask over your mouth and nose. Anyone traveling with small children should attach their own mask first. Then attach your child's mask."

Attach your own mask first? I thought as I leaned back in my seat.

My natural response would have been to put the mask on my child first. Wasn't that what I was always doing—taking care of others and not taking care of myself? Weren't their needs more important than mine? In that moment I realized that if my own personal tank was empty, I'd have nothing to give my children and husband.

During that flight, God showed me the importance of taking care of my own needs. I knew it wouldn't be easy to change, but I was ready to learn.

Janet learned an important lesson. If she didn't take care of her own emotional, physical, and spiritual needs, she'd have nothing left to give her family. Yet how does a mother find time to take care of herself when her children's needs are so demanding and constant? Like Janet, most of us wonder, *Are you kidding? There is no time for me!*

The following is taken from Jeanne Pallos' book *The Circle of Love*. Jeanne suggests that as you read, you take a notepad and a pencil and work through the following exercise:

- Name your most immediate needs. Be honest with yourself. "I need more sleep; I need time to shower, wash my hair, get a haircut, and take care of my personal grooming; I need some new clothes; I need help with housework, laundry, and shopping; I need someone to talk to who understands what I'm going through; I need time to myself; I need exercise; or I need to eat better." Whatever you feel you need, write it down.
- Evaluate the need. After you have listed your needs, determine what kind of need you have. Is this a physical or personal need? Is it an emotional need? Is it a spiritual need?

- Share your needs with others. For a spiritual need, call your pastor and ask for help. Find someone who will pray with you. For personal or physical needs, make a plan. If you need to improve your eating habits, have fruit and healthy snacks available when you're on the run. Getting enough sleep can be difficult. Find times during the day when you can rest. Limit your phone time and visitors. Let your answering machine screen calls. Don't feel you have to maintain a perfect house, cook gourmet meals, and run to every activity. For emotional needs, join a support group; find community services that offer what you need; talk to people who understand your situation. Stay away from people who drain your energy and offer unwanted advice. Surround yourself with people who encourage you and help you.
- After you have figured out what your needs are, remember these are your needs and not your family's needs. Make a plan to get at least one of your needs met on a daily basis—even if it's just a ten-minute bubble bath with candles and soft music, or five minutes on the phone with a friend.
- Taking care of yourself is not being selfish. It is self-preservation. You must preserve your own physical, emotional, and spiritual health in order to meet the needs of your family.
- Now make a list of everything you do right! Tell yourself that you are doing the best you can do. And that's enough.

As Janet learned an important lesson in how to care for her own needs, Tari Stanford helps her daughter face her deepest fear in "No One Will Want to Marry Me!"

No One Will Want to Marry Me!
TARI STANFORD

"Why do I have to have cerebral palsy?" asked my ten-year-old daughter, Genna, as she threw herself across her bed sobbing. "Don't you understand? No one will want to marry me!"

I don't remember what prompted this particular meltdown, but I sat on her bed, wrapped my arms around her, and tried to comfort her. I fought tears as memories flooded my mind.

Genna was born two-and-a-half months premature and was diagnosed with mild cerebral palsy. I say "mild" simply because she can talk and walk, moving all her limbs—but it's labored. Her leg braces make her stand out a bit and appear different from other kids, but her courage and spunk match her classmates.

As I held Genna in my arms, she fell asleep. I remembered back to when she was in second grade. It was the first time she realized others saw her differently—saw her limitations. I was standing with Genna outside her classroom that morning, waiting for the teacher to arrive. As the children lined up, a little red-haired girl passed out birthday invitations to several of the girls. I watched her as she walked by Genna and glanced back. Turning around, she looked me in the eyes and said, "The reason I didn't invite Genna is because she can't skate, and I'm having a roller skating party."

Being caught off guard, I took a deep breath. Did this little girl truly think she was helping the matter by blurting out an explanation?

Genna stood silently by as tears welled up in her eyes. I don't know who was more stunned by this girl's rudeness, Genna or I. I wanted to yell at that little girl in defense of my daughter but knew I needed to comfort Genna instead. Plus, I didn't want to draw attention to an already disastrous situation.

As in other encounters, Genna lived through that situation. I'm sure it also prepared her for future ones, but oh, it hurt both of us.

Softly I laid Genna's head on her pillow. Still sitting by her side and reminiscing, I thought back to the many times during her life when I wanted to blame someone for her troubled birth and subsequent cerebral palsy. I once tried to blame the doctors who delivered her, but it wasn't their fault I went into labor early. I looked at what I did and didn't do during my pregnancy, but I hadn't done anything differently from my first two healthy pregnancies.

I soon realized that there was no one to blame. Instead, I turned to God to help us deal with our day-by-day challenges. I knew that life for Genna would be difficult. Yet I also knew that God promised to heal the heartbreak of a little girl who didn't get invited to a roller skating party.

I took my hand and brushed my fingers along Genna's face. Again I wished my daughter didn't have these problems. "Genna, my love," I whispered softly, "I'm here for you. I'm choosing to be positive and look at the bright side of any circumstance we encounter. And I'm going to believe that one day a Christian guy will see your true beauty inside and out. But whatever happens in your future, I know that you'll always be surrounded by God's strong and loving arms."

Like Genna's mom, we've got to accept the facts and, at the same time, help our kids look ahead to a promising future. We can't let them dwell on the *what-if*s. "What-if no one wants to marry me? What-if I never get asked to a party?"

The *what-if*s are deadly. They can crush our spirits and smother our hope. They carry our thoughts and imaginations to places we will never visit. They take us to places where God isn't.

Albert Einstein knew what the *what-if*s were all about. He pondered them pertaining to his inventions, and today we pay attention to his scientific data and his famous words: "I think and think for months and years. Ninety-nine times, the conclusion is false. The hundredth time I am right."

It is possible to teach our children to dream dreams and not worry. We can show them that "today is the tomorrow they worried about yesterday." We can teach them to follow their dreams and not give up.

Sabrina Coleman learned that when all else fails, she needs to try again. She learned that if she got up one more time than she fell—she would find herself "Running Again."

Running Again
SABRINA COLEMAN

My leg was amputated at the age of eight due to cancer. It took some getting used to, but I didn't let that slow me down. I learned to roller skate on my first prosthesis. In seventh grade I was fitted for a new prosthesis. "We'll put a running strap in it," they said. How was I to know that this running strap was simply a fancy name for an elastic band? I was certain that this "running strap" would give me the ability to run again. I took them at their word and approached my PE teacher, Mrs. Ganns, and asked her to coach me.

"Running?" she questioned. "Sabrina, if you think you can run, I know I can support you!" Thus began my training with Mrs. Ganns to learn to run. What I didn't realize was that no one expected me to run again, except of course, my PE teacher and me.

I continued to practice, and Mrs. Ganns continued to encourage me. Many times I fell to the ground only to have to find ways to bring my body back to its feet. Months went by. Yet with each month I was able to add additional steps to my gait. I kept my running a secret from my parents until I had a full foot-over-foot gaited run. Then I surprised them one day. My parents stood frozen as I ran from the car to the entrance of a restaurant.

"Sabrina," my mom shouted, "you can run!"

My running led me into playing softball. I played first base and left field. When I was up to bat, I knew I had to whack the ball to be able to make it to first base in time. I loved every moment of the game.

Again I was fitted for a new prosthesis, but I was not yet feeling comfortable with my new leg. In between innings of a game, I ran up to the backstop, latched onto the chain link fence, and shouted up into the stands, "Hey, Mom, please go home and get my other leg."

My mom cupped her hands around her mouth and yelled, "Sabrina, you're doing fine with that one. Just go back out and play!"

A person could have heard a pin drop. No one on the opposing team's sidelines realized I had an artificial leg.

When I lost my leg, I didn't let it slow me down, but I did struggle with my thoughts. I had grown up believing in God and attending church. Yet this all stopped when I got cancer. *Why hadn't God prevented the cancer from growing? Did he care I lost my leg?*

During my junior year of high school, a friend invited me to her church. The people were friendly, and it was a great place to socialize. Being mad at God, I went through the motions of prayer without truly praying. My new church friends convinced me to go with them to winter camp. It was there that I broke down and confessed to God all my anger and disappointment. I asked Jesus to come into my broken heart and to become my Savior.

At camp I began to celebrate that the cancer only took my leg and not my life. I made a commitment that God could use me in helping others face and deal with their disabilities. I would walk beside them and tell them that they, too, could run!

Your body cannot heal without play.
Your mind cannot heal without laughter.
Your soul cannot heal without joy.
—CATHERINE RIPPENGER FENWICK

Chapter 10

HEALING THE HEARTBREAK

A Child, a Choice

NANCY C. ANDERSON

I tried to get comfortable on the hard table as the nurse's aide squirted cold sonogram gel on my expanding belly. Two technicians stood at my side. One glided the scope over my bulging stomach, while the other watched the monitor. My eyes focused on the technician studying my baby.

At first her face was expressionless. Then suddenly her eyes grew wide, and her hands flew involuntarily to cover her mouth as she gasped.

"What's wrong?" I asked as I bolted up and repeated my question.

"I'm sorry," she whispered. Trying to compose herself, she scurried toward the door. The other technician followed her out the door.

I tumbled off the table and went to look at the still picture that was on the screen. I didn't see anything unusual. It just looked like a blurry negative of a skinny baby. I said to my unborn child, "I think we're in trouble."

After the amniocentesis, my husband, Ron, and I went back to the hospital for the test results. When we met with the doctor, he spoke to us as if he was reading from a textbook: "Trisomy 18 is a genetic disorder that always involves profound mental retardation and severe disfigurement." Then he said the words that still live inside a tiny zipped pocket in my brain, "Your baby's condition is incompatible with life. Most women in your position, in order to spare themselves unnecessary anguish, just get an abortion. We can schedule one for tomorrow morning."

I wasn't able to speak. I could barely catch my breath. My head was spinning. After an uncomfortable period of silence, Ron and I left the office without saying a word.

That afternoon, I prayed, "Lord, I believe abortion is wrong, but I don't want to go through 'unnecessary anguish.' I don't have the strength to fall in love with a baby who's going to die."

As I prayed, I remembered that the Lord could have chosen to avoid the horrific anguish of the cross. What-if he had taken the easy way out? I saw that the value of his gift was measured by the greatness of his suffering. I told him, with renewed strength, "I offer my pain to you as a gift. I will not abort this child."

I kept saying it, even before I meant it. "I choose to love this baby with all my heart." I willed my words into action. In faith, I moved my hands as I timidly caressed my stomach. In faith, I moved my lips as I mouthed the words, "I love you." Yet, no sound came out. I kept repeating the phrase until my brain found the secret passageway to my heart, and I was free to taste the bittersweet tears of loving a child who would never love me.

My mother gave me some valuable advice, "Try not to think about the future. Your baby is alive today—be alive with him. Treasure every moment."

I talked to him, sang lullabies to him, and prayed for him. I gave him gentle massages through my skin. I knew I had to do my best mothering before he was born.

Four months later we met little Timmy face-to-face. The nurse covered his fragile, twenty-ounce body in a soft blue blanket and matching cap. His heart monitor beeped an unsteady greeting as she handed him to me.

I was surprised by his beautiful little rosebud mouth. It was an oasis of perfection. We held our emotions in check, knowing we had to pour a lifetime of love into a minuscule cup. Ron and I took turns rocking him as we repeatedly told him, "We love you, Timmy." He never opened his eyes. His heart beat slower and slower, and then, reluctantly, it stopped.

We introduced him to his Heavenly Father, "Holy God, here is our son. Thank you for the gift of his precious life and for the privilege of being his parents. We release him into your healing arms."

Then we cried.

Jeanne Pallos read Nancy's story and wrote the following:

Nancy and her husband, Ron, had a choice. They could abort their unborn child, as the doctor recommended, or put their trust in God and receive this child as a gift. No one welcomes pain and anguish, but Nancy chose to love and nurture her unborn child, heeding her mother's wise words: "Your baby is alive today—be alive with him."

Before Timmy was born, Nancy was able to bond with her unborn child and grieve for the child she would lose. At his birth, Nancy experienced the joy of meeting her precious child. Yet she immediately surrendered him back to God.

Nancy and Ron gave meaning and value to their son's short life. They welcomed him into their hearts and ushered him into God's waiting arms. The doctor had suggested they abort and forget. They chose to embrace, love, and remember. Timmy was their child, and he'd always have a place in his parents' hearts.

By facing their loss and acknowledging Timmy's short life, Nancy and Ron experienced closure. They faced their loss with courage and honesty and were able to move forward without regrets.

What happens when a family chooses to forget the existence of a child with special needs? Lauren Briggs shares her experience of losing two special brothers, and like Nancy and Ron, she also knows "What It Is to Hurt."

What It Is to Hurt

LAUREN BRIGGS

"What would a young girl like you know about suffering?" former Secretary of the Interior James Watt asked me at the Christian Bookseller's Association Convention. He listened as I told him my experiences. After a short time, he said, "That's enough. I believe you know what it is to hurt."

For me, hurting began early in life and centered on the thing I wanted most—to be a mother. I treated my dolls as though they were my babies. Pitiful Pearl was my favorite because she looked like she needed to be loved. When I was four, a new real live baby arrived. I was thrilled to have Marita instead of just a doll. Every morning I helped my mother heat Marita's bottle, feed her, and change her diapers. Then I'd watch her to make sure she didn't get into any trouble.

About a year and a half after Marita's arrival, my parents brought home a new baby. Freddie had Dad's beautiful blue eyes, pale blonde hair, and gorgeous dimples.

I helped my mother care for Freddie just as I had Marita—feeding, rocking, and changing him. But when he was six months old, we realized that he wasn't progressing the way a normal child should. He began screaming in the middle of the night. Mother and I would meet in the hallway, running to help him. All I could think was, *My baby is hurting.*

Mother and I took turns holding his stiffened body, pacing the floor until he eventually relaxed and returned to sleep. These nightly sessions finally sent us to the doctor's office. I held Freddie in the waiting room until it was our turn to enter, then stood anxiously in the background while Dr. Granger, the pediatrician, examined him. After conferring with a neurologist, Dr. Granger told Mother, "I don't know how to tell you this, but your son is hopelessly brain damaged. You might as well put him away, forget about him, and maybe have another child."

Our baby hopeless? I couldn't believe it! I kept asking myself, *Why did this have to happen? Why wasn't my baby brother going to be like all the other children I'd seen?* Mother and Dad had always taught me to work hard and that I could do almost anything I wanted. But here was something no amount of work could change. Unknown to my parents, following that discovery, I hid in my room and cried.

Doctors reassured my parents that this would never happen again, so they decided to have another child. A year and a half later, Larry was born. In the meantime, caring for Freddie, who was having ten to twelve convulsions a day, was becoming increasingly difficult. While Mother was in the hospital delivering Larry, Dad put Freddie into a private children's hospital where he could receive round-the-clock care.

At the time I had no idea what had happened to Freddie. He just disappeared.

I never saw him again. Five months after he was institutionalized, he died of pneumonia.

Both Mother and I put all our efforts into nurturing Larry to ensure nothing could go wrong with him. We never discussed our enormous feelings of hurt and deprivation over losing Freddie. We just prayed that Larry would be everything Freddie couldn't be.

One week after Freddie died, Mother went into Larry's room to wake him from his nap, but he just lay there expressionless and limp. Terrified that the nightmare was repeating itself, I insisted on accompanying Mother to the doctor's office. After he examined Larry, Dr. Granger turned to Mother. "I can't believe it. He's got the same thing. He's hopelessly brain damaged."

I felt sick inside. *Isn't there something we can do?* I kept thinking over and over.

Mother spoke up, "We caught this one earlier. Maybe there's some hope."

But there was no hope. Larry grew steadily worse. Surgery when he was one year old revealed that his brain was a nonfunctioning mass.

"No hope!" I cried when I saw Larry's bandaged head, swollen beyond recognition. *How could this happen a second time?*

Blind and deaf, Larry never grew or changed after his surgery. His crying and convulsions continued.

One afternoon as I was playing at a friend's house, I glanced out the window to see Mother and Dad backing out of the driveway. I ran outside in time to find out that they were taking Larry to the same children's hospital where Freddie had died one year before.

I could see that these traumas were devastating my parents, so I kept most of my feelings to myself. When kids at school called my brothers "morons," I never told Mother and Dad. No one knew how personally I'd taken these losses or how much I missed my two brothers.

My parents never mentioned the babies again, and we tried desperately to pretend we'd never had them. Since Larry was nothing but a living vegetable, Dad decided it was best that we not see him again and just remember him as he'd been. Privately, though, I would think of both Freddie and Larry often. I'd remember their birth dates. How old would Freddie be? How old would Larry be?

Contrary to the doctors' predictions that Larry would die before his fifth birthday, he lived to be nineteen years old. When he died, he was still the same size he had been when he was a year old. He never developed at all.

Even though I was a mother myself by then, his death was far more difficult for me than I anticipated. Although he hadn't been an integral part of our home, he was my brother. I had to grieve for him. His death was especially hard for me because I was trying to discover the cause of my brothers' illness. But when Larry died, I gave up hope of finding out if his condition was hereditary. I stepped out in faith and had three children of my own—all healthy and perfectly normal.

The words pierced Lauren's heart: "What would a young girl like you know about suffering?" Outwardly, Lauren appeared to have a perfect life. No pain. No loss. That was the life her parents tried to give her as a child. Yet as an adult, Lauren yearned for the brothers she had lost in childhood. If only she'd had a chance to say good-bye.

Lauren's parents felt they were protecting her from pain by removing Freddie and Larry from the home. The family had experienced great loss, but no one talked about it. In fact, the family acted as if these two children had never been born.

Today Lauren is a woman who reflects on her experience and talks about her pain as a child. She offers insight and understanding for helping children cope with the illness or death of a sibling. Lauren's message is one of healing and hope.

Jeanne Pallos suggests the following ways to help children deal with loss:

- Be honest with your children.
- Use age-appropriate language to help children understand what is happening.
- Listen to their fears, hurts, anger, and concerns.
- Learn to use words that encourage them to talk about their feelings: "How does that make you feel?" "Do you want to talk about it?" "Is there anything I can do to help you feel better?" "Thank you for telling me that. You are a very brave person." "I know you are hurting, but I'm always here for you." "It's OK to cry."
- Help children say good-bye to the person they have lost: write a letter, draw a picture, or write a poem.
- Celebrate the memory of the person they have lost: plant a tree, make a special garden, donate to a charity, make a scrapbook of memories, blow bubbles on a windy hill, or fly a kite with the person's name attached to the string.
- Keep the person's picture in a place of honor.
- Talk about that person on special days, such as that person's birthday.
- Laugh and remember the good times together.

Children need to know it's OK to grieve. God uses the adults in their lives to bring healing. As you minister to your child, may God bring healing to your own hurting heart.

Charlotte Adelsperger wrote the book *When Your Child Hurts*. In it she shares how she found comfort in her time of need through "A Signal at Night."

A Signal at Night
CHARLOTTE ADELSPERGER

The local hospital had become my temporary home. There, John, our precious eighteen-month-old son, struggled with a respiratory infection. The first few days my husband or I stood by his crib, watching each of his breaths. I literally trembled in fear as I saw his rapid breathing and ballooning chest. The days were long, and the nights seemed endless. Yet with intravenous antibiotics, breathing treatments, and many prayers, John's health began to improve.

I thanked God with my whole heart for John's recovery. Yet I was both ecstatic and emotionally drained. I felt exhausted from the nights I stayed awake, tending to my young son. And now, trying to sleep on a reclining chair in John's hospital room brought nothing but misery. I was ready for a break. I missed our little three-year-old, Karen, and my husband, Bob.

Karen and I chatted by phone several times a day. Hearing her high-pitched voice say, "Mommy, I miss you" tore at my heart. I ached to be home again to hold Karen on my lap and read her a favorite story. I longed to spend time with my husband. I despised the fact that we now seemed to pass in the halls as we rotated our shifts at home, at work, and with John.

One afternoon I sat next to John as he slept. Thinking about how truly difficult our situation was, I began to feel sorry for myself. Within moments Bob walked through the door. My restlessness poured itself into chatter. I briefed my husband regarding John's latest medical evaluation. We both delighted in his steady improvement. Quickly Bob told me about the cute things Karen was doing and how things were at his job.

All too soon Bob glanced at his watch. "I really have to go," he said. "Karen's waiting for me." He then gave me a long hug and kissed me gently.

"I don't want you to leave," I said, my eyes filling with tears, "but I know you must." How I wished our whole family could be together again.

Bob gave me another hug. "Look down there," he said, pointing through the window to where his car was parked. "I'll drive right past your room. You stand here at the window. When I come by, I'll blink my lights. It'll be my little signal that I love you, and I'll be thinking of you."

Minutes later I recognized our car as it slowly moved down the street below. The lights flashed on, then off. It moved a few more feet; then my husband blinked the lights again. As Bob turned onto the main street, I saw another blink. The lights kept flashing on and off until my blurred eyes could no longer see them.

Still standing at the window, I looked up in the sky and noticed the stars. One by one I saw them blink. My Father in heaven had also found a way to remind me that he loves me and is thinking of me. *I love you. I love you. I love you,* the stars twinkled. Isn't this the signal God wants all of his children to see every night?

God loves us. Not only did he use the stars to communicate his love to Charlotte, but years ago he used a star to prove his love for us as he led the magi to his infant Son, Jesus.

One father said, "When my heartache is great and I fear for my child's future, I've learned to look up into the night sky. There I see the stars and am reminded of the One who placed them there. Then I know that all is well."

Brook, too, learned to use signs as a way of communicating. He used his hands and body language instead of his voice. Zel shares the story of Brook, his grandson, in "Our Angelman."

Our Angelman
ZEL BROOKS

There was no one else in the emergency waiting room when we pushed in our wheelchair-bound fourteen-year-old grandson, Brook, who had an undiagnosed disability since birth. Time seemed to stand still as the nurse recorded our intake information. Brook had received reconstructive surgery on his left foot and ankle a week earlier, and a pungent odor emitting from the cast told us the foot had become infected.

While we were waiting, a man entered, pushing an elderly woman in a wheelchair. "My mother's having a heart attack!" he exclaimed. We stepped aside, realizing they would be taken care of first.

Brook kept pulling at the cast above his toes, unable to verbalize his pain. My wife, Leah, cuddled him in her arms and murmured, "I know it hurts, Brookie. How can Oomah make it better?" Oomah was Brook's nickname for his grandmother.

The answer was immediate. Using sign language, he touched each palm with the opposite index finger, signing "Jesus."

We responded with his favorite chorus, "Jesus loves me, this I know, for the Bible tells me so. . . ."

Brook laughed and clapped. His whole body shook with delight, hands raised as we sang. Predictably, his signed response was, "More!" Of course, we had to sing it again, accompanied by excited clapping from our precious grandson.

By this time in Brook's life, hospitals had become a second home to him and to us. His heart surgery at eight months, two years on an apnea monitor, air ambulance flights, and multiple other surgeries left our family feeling overwhelmed. We thought it was almost more than one family could take, even though Leah and I helped with Brook as much as time would permit.

Unfortunately, our daughter, Kapri, and her husband exhausted the lifetime limit on Brook's health insurance in the first year. A long series of frustrations, all too familiar to families of kids with special needs, followed. Agencies and schools that serve "special" children employ many dedicated professionals, but large organizations foster bureaucracy and mindless errors, which compromise timely care.

On his fourteenth birthday Brook still had received no clear diagnosis, although the infection in his foot was quickly cleared up with antibiotics after this trip to the emergency room.

Six months after this incident, a diagnosis was finally reached: Brook had Angelman syndrome—a disease that caused developmental delays, minimal or no speech, seizures, movement and balance disorders, a short attention span, and frequent laughing and smiling.

We found that we were no longer alone. Brook's mother scoured the Internet and found more than five thousand other families struggling with this little-known disease discovered by Dr. Harry Angelman in 1965.

Even though Brook's speech is limited, his signing and his expressive face communicate effectively. When he thrusts out a hand, he means "shake my hand." He's a great mimic. And just because he can't speak doesn't mean he has nothing to say!

The most priceless moments with Brook are during worship. Praise choruses bring out the best in him. His infectious grin and laughter lead others to celebrate God's gift of life. His sparkling eyes and handshake invite unpretentious fellowship. And nothing turns Brook on like the name *Jesus*. He touches each palm with the opposite index finger, signing "Jesus." Then his hands fly up and he smiles.

We never imagined, during the anxiety and discouragement of Brook's fragile infancy, what joy he would provide. Brook is our Angelman.

∞

Yes, the sun always rises, even after the darkest night. Our open wounds of grief and despair heal, and we are able to see what we couldn't see before. Linda Evans Shepherd says, "When your handicapped child first enters your life, you are blinded by pain. But your sight returns as you can see how precious is the gift God has given you."

Charlene Derby experienced a dark time in her life—a time when her dreams were shaken and reality hit hard. Yet daybreak came, and she also saw what she had not seen before. Charlene tells her story in "Finding a New Life."

Finding a New Life
CHARLENE A. DERBY

Twelve years ago I thought my life was wonderful. I had a witty, intelligent husband; a challenging job; and a house in the suburbs. Plus, after ten years of marriage, I was finally pregnant. I didn't think things could get much better.

There were no complications at birth, and as we watched our son grow from infancy into a toddler, we had few worries. In many ways he seemed like his father and me. We could tell he was smart, but he'd never be a star athlete. We were sure he'd grow up with a sense of humor, an important commodity in our family. Little did we know how much we'd need that gift over the next few years.

Our first surprise came when Brad's preschool teacher told us she didn't think he was ready for kindergarten. "Boys develop later than girls," she explained. "I think he'd benefit from a 'bonus year.'" We agonized over this decision. We knew Brad was smart, but we didn't want to push him. So we reluctantly agreed to a second year of preschool. Many of our friends supported us in this decision.

Our second surprise came at the end of kindergarten. "Brad's writing is illegible," the teacher told us during our parent-teacher conference. "His coloring is poor, and his worksheets are messy. I suggest you find ways to work on his fine motor skills."

When I discussed this with a friend, she suggested an eye exam. I took her advice, and we discovered that Brad was very farsighted. We bought glasses for him and expected that once he got used to them he'd begin to realize his potential.

Our third surprise came during Brad's first-grade parent-teacher conference. "You might want to get your son tested," the teacher advised. "He could possibly have attention deficit or a language processing problem." Without pausing, she continued to explain the behaviors she'd observed, which weren't at all consistent with the picture of a bright boy we had in our heads! With her help we initiated a series of assessments.

By the end of Brad's second-grade year, with teacher, therapist, and psychologist opinions overflowing, we had what we thought was a thorough analysis of Brad's academic and social needs. We were given labels like "nonverbal learning disability," "visual motor learning disability," "pervasive developmental delay," and "autistic spectrum disorder." We began to feel that life was a multiple-choice question, and we didn't know which answer to pick.

After consulting with friends and further exploring the learning disabilities diagnosis, we decided to approach Brad's needs from an educational perspective. He began third grade in a private school designed for students with language-based learning differences. He also participated in occupational therapy, vision therapy, and speech for pragmatic language classes. There haven't been any more surprises.

Now, as Brad participates in his fifth-grade class, we are beginning to see the light at the end of the tunnel. While he may need academic accommodations for the remainder of his school career, he's become a happy, well-adjusted boy. He's active in Cub Scouts, getting good grades, and playing the flute in the school band.

Me? I lost a corporate job and found a rewarding career as the mother of a child with special educational needs. I lost the sense of security offered by a suburban lifestyle and found security in a God who is faithful, no matter where our walk with him takes us. I lost the perception that special needs are disgraceful and found the grace demonstrated by God's commitment to diversity.

And my husband? He still has a sense of humor.

Charlene has found that God is faithful. Through the past few years she has learned to live day by day, trusting him to meet the needs of her son. She has allowed God to mold her and to help her be the mother her son needs. Charlene was willing to give up life as she knew it and become a "Waiting Room Mom." How blessed she is!

Waiting Room Mom

CHARLENE A. DERBY

She wanted to be a soccer mom.
She even loved pizza.
She loved being outside,
But she's inside—a waiting room mom.

She's waiting,
Waiting inside
For a doctor's diagnosis,
A psychologist's sentence,
A therapist's treatise,
A tutor's sympathy.

She hates the charade of pretending
That therapy is play,
That the tutor's tools are toys,
That this is a "normal" childhood for her active boy.

Yet she waits
And prays,
Knowing that the most effective intervention
Is the work of the Holy Spirit
In the life of her family.

Then the towhead bursts into the waiting room
Eager to head home.
"Great! He did great today!"
She hears as she's dragged out the door.

She winks at the boy, bouncing in the backseat.
"Hey, buddy," she whispers,
"Shall we pick up a pizza for dinner?"

"That'd be great, Mom," he says. "Just great!"

*We are all pencils in the hand of a writing God,
who is sending love letters to the world.*
—MOTHER TERESA

Chapter 11

RECEIVING UNEXPECTED BLESSINGS

Plum Purple City Lights
JANET LYNN MITCHELL

"Mom, I've found exactly what I want for Christmas! It will look great in my room!"

Wanting to buy her what she truly desired, I hurried to the store to buy Jenna's 1990 Christmas present—a thirteen-foot wallpaper mural of Manhattan's skyline. In just weeks my sixteen-year-old daughter's bedroom took on a new look. The nightlights of the Manhattan Bridge, the Empire State Building, and the Twin Towers stretched across her wall. Curtains, a bedspread, and a lamp were the added touches to convert Jenna's California hideaway into the glittering lights of New York City.

Truthfully, I did not share Jenna's taste in interior design. We had spent hours together shopping and contemplating different ways in which she could redecorate her room. I'd shown her flowers in pinks and yellows, and she again escorted me back to the store to take "one more look" at lower Manhattan at dusk, fashioned in plum purple and blues.

"It's cool, Mom. I love it! Can't you see? The city is alive, and its lights reflect off the water a silhouette of the New York skyline. Look! There are even two American flags flying proudly."

I saw them. The two American flags were the size of small safety pins. And to me, the mural reflected a busy city, full of action and little peace. Nevertheless, this was for Jenna's room. Thus I quickly resolved that any flowers Jenna may ever display would be in a vase!

Like many moms, each night since she was born I've eased my way into my daughter's room. I ask Jenna about her day and listen to her dreams of the future. I've also sat waiting patiently for the results of her last blood test of the day—praying that her blood sugar levels would be in the safety range for her to go to sleep and then determining how much insulin she would need to take to get her through the night.

During our moments of medical management, we've often sat studying the skyline, pointing out different places we someday want to visit. Night after night Jenna and I have surveyed different buildings and skyscrapers, pondering what their occupants might have done that day. Night after night I'd point to the Twin Towers, sometimes even laying my hand across them saying, "Let's pray for the people who work there."

Jenna always responded, "Mom, I pray for them every night!"

It's now years later. Life in New York City has drastically changed since September 11, 2001, and so has the view of the skyline. But Jenna's room remains unchanged. The Twin Towers still stand tall, adhered to Jenna's wall. Those two little flags the size of safety pins remain untouched, declaring our freedom.

I now see what wasn't clear when I purchased the wallpaper mural. It's more than OK for moms and daughters to differ in their likes. For it is God who gave Jenna her taste of interior design and her desire for a wall mural of Manhattan. And for an entire year before 9/11, despite Jenna's own need for a healing touch from God, she prayed for people she didn't know and for a city she'd never seen. How grateful I am that I quickly gave in to her desires. Putting my dreams of flowers to bed, I allowed Jenna the freedom to follow her heart.

I still find my way to Jenna's room each night. She tests her blood as we talk about her day and her plans for tomorrow. Yet, just before I kiss her goodnight, a lump forms in my throat. I try to speak as I point toward Jenna's wall mural.

"I know, Mom," she whispers while gazing at her wall, "I'm still praying."

⚭

A combination of Jenna's sensitive heart and the New York City skyline that surrounds her when she sleeps prompted her to pray for the people of New York City. Little did Jenna know before 9/11 how needed her prayers were or how many lives would be touched because she prayed.

All of us who love children with special needs have the same opportunity to pray and to be intercessors for other families we meet along the way. We can never underestimate the power of prayer. One mother said, "I can't pass one bald child in the cancer ward without praying for him and his family."

Another said, "I pray for the children with special needs who are mainstreamed in my daughter's class. I pray that the teasing is little and their strength is great!" A third said, "A stranger held me in her arms as my child was whisked away to the operating room, a stranger who led me straight to my Father God in prayer."

When those of us who love children with special needs find ourselves praying, we are blessed beyond words. Joanne Schulte has written about her friend Kelly Clauss. Kelly prayed, God heard, and many were blessed. Joanne shares about "A Baby Who Changed a Mommy."

The Baby Who Changed a Mommy
JOANNE SCHULTE

The stop-and-go traffic was terrible that day as Kelly ran errands in her new SUV. In spite of it, she couldn't help rejoicing over how good God was to her. She had the support of a Christian husband, ample finances, two healthy boys—and now she was five months pregnant.

But if God took it all away, she thought, *how would I respond?* Suddenly the traffic stopped. There was the deafening screech of brakes and tires, the sound of metal against metal, the impact . . . that terrible jolt.

Kelly never liked hospitals, but now she was in the emergency room. She didn't think she had been hurt, yet the technician kept checking the ultrasound over and over again. Finally she asked, "Why is it taking so long to check on my baby? Is everything OK?"

The diagnosis came at last. "Your baby's right kidney is not functioning, and it will need to come out eventually," the doctor said.

Baby Brian was born six weeks premature, and thus began his medical problems, one after another: double pneumonia, breathing and heart problems, respiratory scentia virus, and severe gastrointestinal problems. At four months old, his nonfunctioning kidney was removed.

The beautiful life Kelly had enjoyed soon took an unwelcome turn. Her husband, unable to deal with Brian's health problems, blocked out serious communication between them. Financial problems arose and strained their marriage. This was a brief and difficult time in their lives.

"Lord, it seems like you've taken everything away! How did things get so bad?" she kept asking. "How did they get so bad?" One night, unable to sleep, she knelt by her bed and prayed, "Lord, I don't know how to deal with all of this. I only know you say to praise you in all things, so Lord, I praise you, and I will continue to do so no matter what happens."

Brian was seeing doctors almost weekly. One day in the doctor's office, Kelly noticed a woman's sick baby. Kelly's heart ached for her as they talked together. She felt helpless as she listened to the struggles in this girl's life. It was a defining moment.

Kelly left the doctor's office, determined somehow to make a difference in the lives of other mothers like this woman. "I'm not sure how it will happen, Lord," she prayed, "but I believe this is your will, and I know nothing is too difficult for you."

That Sunday her pastor said, "Fifty people in the audience have special stickers under their chairs. Please bring them to me." Kelly took her sticker to the pastor, not knowing what would happen. The pastor gave each person an envelope containing one hundred dollars and said, "Use this money to make a difference for God's kingdom."

She immediately thought of the young woman in the doctor's office and the many mothers she had talked to in the neonatal and pediatric intensive care units of the hospital. She remembered the agony and hopelessness on their faces and the pain in their hearts.

Kelly wanted to buy Bibles with that money and give them to hurting women. Instead, she came across a mother in need and decided to give it all to her. But having learned of Kelly's desire to give away Bibles, a publisher began supplying her with boxes of free Bibles.

Then, with the encouragement of her husband, she began a ministry. Today Kelly and some of her friends underline Bible verses that offer encouragement and hope as well as verses that tell how to have a personal relationship with Jesus Christ. She works with referrals from doctors as well as requests from individuals. Kelly visits women hospitalized with pregnancy-related problems and those who have babies with special needs. Her visits are brief, but she always assures these women she understands their pain and just wants to bring them love and encouragement. Before she leaves, she gives each one a Bible with the underlined verses.

Brian still has serious health issues, and Kelly still doesn't care for hospitals. Yet she goes there often, each time praying she will be a blessing to women like herself who know what it means to live with children with special needs.

Kelly prayed and then put her faith into action. God used Kelly's own circumstances and heartache to bring comfort and blessings to other mothers she didn't know. Strangers became friends, and friends became fellow sisters in Christ.

Sometimes God calls us to step out of our comfort zone and reach out to others with compassion. To underline Scripture verses and give a Bible to someone whose heart is breaking can be such a blessing. To take a couple of minutes out of our day to pray for those we don't know, nor will ever meet, takes very little time, yet it can have eternal ramifications.

Linda Evans Shepherd has firsthand experience in stepping out of her comfort zone without making her daughter uncomfortable. Like many families with "special" children, we are all "Discovering Common Ground."

Discovering Common Ground
LINDA EVANS SHEPHERD

Even though my daughter, Laura, is severely disabled and can only communicate through tongue signals, she is like other girls her age in many ways. Therefore, her mother has the power to embarrass her terribly!

The first time I discovered this was when she was in pre-school. Laura's teacher thought it would be a good idea for me to come with Laura and explain her handicaps to the other kids. As I finished explaining Laura's limitations, wheelchair, and life-support system, my eyes met hers, and I knew Laura felt mortified. I thought she'd never forgive me.

A few years later Laura's second-grade teacher peered above her glasses to explain I needed to come into the classroom to talk to Laura's classmates about my daughter. I felt concerned, and so did Laura. What could I say to the kids that wouldn't embarrass my sensitive child?

The morning came, and Laura frowned as I walked into her class, which was already in progress. "Laura," I asked, "would you like to come to the front of the room with me as I talk to your friends?"

Laura sat in her purple wheelchair and made a pointed "no" sign with her tongue. Then she shut her eyes.

I hesitated. This was going to be tougher than I had thought. "I'm Laura's mom," I started out, addressing the typical children, "and I want to tell you something about Laura."

At that point Laura stuck out her lower lip.

"I just want all of you to know how much Laura's dad, brother, and I love her."

Her tightly shut eyes fluttered.

"I want you to know how glad we are Laura is our little girl."

A slight smile spread across Laura's pretty face, and she peeked out of one eye.

A little boy raised his hand and asked hesitantly, "How come Laura is in a wheelchair?"

Laura squeezed her eyes shut as I said, "You know, Laura doesn't like for me to talk about that. But let me say Laura was hurt in a car accident. How many of you have ever been hurt and had to go to the hospital?"

Twenty children raised their hands, all eager to share their stories.

"Wow," I said with surprise, "that's almost everyone." I noticed Laura peeking again, and I continued, "So most of you can understand what Laura went through."

A little girl dressed in pink pants and a matching teddy-bear print T-shirt raised her hand. "I just want you to know we all love Laura very much."

The other children nodded their agreement.

Eyes wide open, Laura grinned from ear to ear.

By the end of my time with the children, Laura was still smiling and greatly relieved her mom had not embarrassed her.

Until that day Laura did not know how many ways she was like her friends. And I learned how much the other children identified with and loved her. What an exciting surprise!

The children proved that Jesus' challenge in John 13:34, "Just as I have loved you, you should also love one another," meant more to them than just a nice thought.

Love can bridge the impossible. Through the eyes of love, children can find acceptance, and parents can find ways to meet their child's needs. When John Vonhof volunteered as a counselor at a family camp for children with disabilities, he planned to share his time and his love with some of God's special children. Yet what John found was that he was blessed and loved in return. He shares his story in "Little John, Big John."

Little John, Big John
JOHN VONHOF

The first thing that caught my eye was not his electric wheelchair, his arms that seemed to flop around as he talked, the way his head leaned to one side, or the crooked shape of his hands and fingers. It was the smile on his face and the way he looked at me. I realized he was not a typical kid.

This encounter took place the first day of the family camp for children with disabilities, and I didn't know anyone there. The dining room was crowded, and few seats were left. Jonathan and his mother were sitting at the dinner table, and the seat across from them was empty. I decided to join them.

Six-year-old Jonathan has cerebral palsy, the type commonly called athetoid, meaning he's wiggly with rapid, random, jerky motions. As he gets older, it will be harder for him to control his body's movement.

Jonathan and I talked throughout dinner. He asked me a lot of questions, and I asked him many in return. I don't remember most of them, but I do remember the most important one.

"Whaaat'ss youuur naaaaamee?" he asked in a halting and drawn out sentence. His face and body twitched, continually moving as he said the simple three words.

"John. What's your name?"

As he laughed, his head turned from side to side, and the food slid off his fork. There was more food around his plate than on it. "My naaaamee is John toooo. I'mmm liiittle John, youuu'rre biiigg John!" We both laughed some more and continued talking.

His enthusiasm was contagious. His mother said, "The sheer force of his personality puts people at ease, and his joy shines brightly."

Throughout the week Jonathan worked hard to share his joy. This was what he did best. I saw it as the gift with which God has blessed him, and I noticed people always surrounded him. He was never alone. Teens and adults pushed him in his chair. They knelt down to be at his level, and they played games with him. They laughed with him. Everyone who met Jonathan experienced God's joy through him.

The camp was the perfect opportunity to meet children with special needs: Bryce with spina bifida; Michael with a traumatic brain injury; twin sisters, Sara and Jessica, with Down syndrome; and others with physical, mental, visual, and communication disorders. God's love is manifested in all of them.

Yet it was Jonathan who made an indelible impression on me. Little John blessed Big John many times over. We played games and laughed. We talked. He pretended not to see me and then broke out in laughter. We talked some more. Nothing deep—just light conversation between me and a child who just happened to have cerebral palsy.

I could have sat somewhere else that night—perhaps beside a child who looked more "normal." But then I would have missed Jonathan and the blessings he so freely gave. Little John, a small child with special needs, was picked by God to bless someone who thought he was there to help the children.

Charles Swindoll once said:

> The longer I live, the more I realize the impact of atti-
> tude on life. . . . The remarkable thing is, we have a choice
> every day regarding the attitude we will embrace for that day.
> We cannot change our past. . . . We cannot change the fact
> that people will act in a certain way. We cannot change the
> inevitable. The only thing we can do is play on the strings we
> have, and that is our attitude.

Jonathan didn't have control over his bodily movements and functions, but he had control over his attitude. Cerebral palsy bound him to
a wheelchair, but it did not bind his positive, contagious spirit.

Jonathan learned to focus on what he could do and not on what
had been lost. He could smile, laugh, make friends, spread joy, play
games, talk, and be a friend. Because of his attitude, people were drawn
to him. They saw the person, not the disability, and they were blessed.

Like John Vonhof, a father learns from his disabled son's gentle and
generous spirit in the following story, "Bryson's Reward."

Bryson's Reward
LISA TUTTLE

When the newspaper advertised a community Easter egg hunt, Scott
decided to take his three children. Although they arrived at the park a
half hour before the designated start of the hunt, hundreds of children
and parents already milled about the field.

Scott felt a twinge of disappointment as he read the age categories
from the chart. Bryson would compete against six- and seven-year-olds.
At six, he resembled a four-year-old in size and development. Sickly
since birth, Bryson had struggled for every physical accomplishment he
ever achieved. Heart surgery and years of physical therapy had improved
his health, but children his age towered over him in size.

"Good thing we came early," Scott told Bryson, "so you can get a
spot in the front row." Bryson followed his dad to the starting line and
stood with the other children, smiling and eager. Scott left him standing in the front while he walked Bryson's siblings to their locations.

He returned to find Bryson pushed back to the seventh row. Disheartened, he knelt beside the boy. "What happened, buddy? How did you get way back here?"

"The other kids wanted to be up front. They were pushing and shoving, so I let them have my spot. I don't mind being in the back."

Scott sighed. Born with a gentle and generous spirit, Bryson never hesitated to share or give preference to other children, even if it meant sacrificing something important to him.

Knowing the crowd would overpower Bryson, Scott offered the boy a strategy. "When the gun sounds, run as fast as you can down the sideline. The other children will stop to pick up eggs. You run past them and grab eggs from the other end of the field."

Bryson, obedient to a fault, nodded. "OK, Daddy."

Minutes later, the gun exploded, and children ran in every direction, scooping up eggs.

Scott watched Bryson run for a moment before turning to search for his other children. The contest ended in less than two minutes. After they swept the fields clean of their pastel treasures, the children returned to their parents.

Scott's oldest son arrived first, then his daughter. They waited together for Bryson. Other children rushed from the field designated for the six- and seven-year-olds, their bags bulging with eggs. Seeing their bounty, Scott had high expectations of Bryson's success. Soon Bryson came into view.

With a sweet, satisfied smile gracing his lips and chocolaty eyes alight with excitement, he approached their little huddle. Scott's gaze fell upon Bryson's bag. Only a few small lumps lined the bottom. His heart twisted in his chest. Bryson's portion in life was to conduct himself politely when others were pushy, to remember to be considerate and kind when others were rude and aggressive, only to be cheated out of the reward he deserved. At that moment life seemed unfair.

Bryson opened his bag and proudly showed the four eggs he'd collected—a pitiful reward for such innate goodness.

As was Scott's habit, he downplayed the fact that Bryson's performance was not as productive as the other children's. "I'm proud of you for running fast and for being polite," Scott said. "We've had so much fun today, and you collected four eggs!"

Bryson looked down at his scant collection. With his trademark sweet smile, he examined his eggs, rolling them over in his hands. He seemed content with his find.

As the hunt came to a close, the officials asked the contestants to empty their eggs into their sacks and return the plastic shells for use again next year.

Scott knelt down, and the children opened their eggs, exclaiming about the candy as they worked at the task. Bryson, lacking strength in his hands and arms, struggled to pry his eggs apart.

Scott leaned over to assist him. "Let me help you with that, buddy," he said as he opened the first egg.

A slip of paper fluttered to the ground. Bryson picked it up and stared in confusion. "Paper? Why did they put paper in my egg?"

Scott took the slip from him and read: "You are the grand prize winner." Emotion flooded Scott's heart as God reminded him that winning isn't about being the fastest or the strongest. To God, winning is in the attitude.

Bryson went home with a shiny new bike.

Peggy Matthews-Rose says:,

As Bryson's dad understood, we live in a world that applauds winners. Competition is both encouraged and natural, as it spurs us toward excellence. In parenting, we have come to expect that our children should arrive at predetermined benchmarks in life because . . . well, because they all do! But every now and then God gives us an exceptional child, one who does not live or play by the rules. Those children may come with challenges that break our hearts, but God can use them in ways we could never imagine. All it takes is for us to see them through his eyes.

Greg Laurie, in his book *Marriage + Connections*, reminds us that our children are gifts from God, whether they seem like it all the time or not! As such, they are to be treasured. Bryson's dad learned that God loves us just the way we are, even when that way is less than perfect by society's standards.

Pastor Greg also says that these gifts from God are "not ours to be molded but rather to be unfolded. It is our privilege as parents to help them discover the unique individual that God has made them."[1] A wonderful example of one of these gifts is Keith as shown in the story "Birthday Party! Bring Seven Dollars!"

Birthday Party! Bring Seven Dollars!
ANN JAY

At breakfast the Jay family sat around the table discussing Keith's eighteenth birthday party that had taken place the night before. Keith's younger sister, Jana, commented, "Do you think Keith invited the whole town? He sure had a crowd!"

"Maybe he did. Judging from the group that squeezed into our living room last night, Keith didn't miss many people when he issued his invitation," I replied. When the family scattered and went about the day's activities, I lingered at the table thinking about the party and our family's blessings.

Weeks earlier Keith had started encouraging others to join him for his celebration. Because Keith has Down syndrome and a speech problem, his words weren't all there, but his enthusiasm was. It was evident by the number of people who came that he got his point across.

His message went something like this: "Have I got a deal for you! It's a party for me! It's my birthday! We'll have cake, cake with fire on it. I'll be there. You come." Then, using the clearest language of all, he added, "Oh, yes, bring seven dollars."

Even after Dad insisted that Keith shouldn't ask for money, he continued to solicit donations, compromising by asking for only two dollars instead of the seven.

The birthday party was bigger and better than any before. In fact, there was so much celebrating that it took two parties to get in all the fun. For Keith, the festivities began at the high school pep rally when the cheerleaders proclaimed him the "Sweetwater Mustang Number One Fan," an undisputed fact, and the entire student body sang "Happy Birthday" to him.

Keith enthusiastically directed the band (unsolicited), led cheers, and mingled with his idols—the coaches and football players.

Following the pep rally, the team escorted Keith to their locker room, toasted him with punch and cake, and officially declared him an honorary Mustang. Together the players presented him with a team jersey and tugged it over his head. Keith's delight was so intense that bright tears glistened in his eyes. The rest of us looked away to keep from crying too.

The day didn't end there. In the evening Keith's friends, young and old, began to arrive at our home. Many of them came with money, just as Keith had suggested. Each of them came with a story about how Keith had touched his or her life. After the stories about Keith began, they continued one after another. One person told how touched she was when Keith cried when her pet died.

We learned that Keith often brightened the school secretary's day by bringing her little flowers he picked from the front lawn. The man from the grocery store told how Keith watched him sack groceries and always told him, "Good job!" when the last item was sacked. A coach even confessed that he had lost Keith in Austin when they went to the Special Olympics.

Coach Gonzales finally found Keith over at the stadium, practicing for his big run the next day. Coach said, "I was frantic about Keith! I wanted to be really mad at him for leaving the room, but what enthusiasm he has for life! Keith was pursuing his dream, even at midnight, and he won!"

Although each person had a different story to tell about Keith, they all nodded in agreement with one man's summary. Virgil said, "I was shopping in the mall and wham! Somebody jumped on me and hugged me so hard I couldn't breathe. It nearly scared me to death before I realized it was Keith." Then, with obvious joy, Virgil added the crystallizing statement, "No one loves me like Keith does."

My thoughts returned to earlier when I had watched Keith concentrate on folding his money and hiding it in his new briefcase. Even with the reduction in the amount of money he requested, Keith took in a whopping eighty-six dollars. I cried joyful tears.

I remembered Keith's earlier birthdays. As I tried to figure out what made the difference, I realized that I've cried on previous birthdays—but different tears. When Keith was little, for me the day only marked more clearly the things that Keith couldn't do. When he was a year old, he couldn't walk. He was three, and he couldn't talk. He was four, and he wasn't potty trained. He was twelve, and he couldn't write. Even worse, he still couldn't talk.

Now we celebrate. We celebrate what Keith can do. We celebrate the people who teach him. We celebrate the kids at school who make him a part of their lives. We celebrate the people who love him. But mostly, we celebrate Keith and the love and joy that surround him.

Just as I thought I was about to reach a profound truth regarding Keith, he burst into the room, waving his bankroll and exclaiming, "I'm rich! I'm rich!"

Without hesitation, I agreed, "You sure are! You're very rich!" In my heart I realized the wisdom of the biblical truth found in 1 Corinthians 13:13, which I have paraphrased: "The greatest gift of all is love."

I smiled at my son and said, "Keith, you're the richest guy I know!" as I thought to myself, *And so are we!*

Happy birthday, Keith.

---

1. Greg Laurie, *Marriage + Connections: 60 Devotions to Strengthen Your Marriage* (Wheaton, Ill.: Tyndale House, 2002).

> *Thou who hast given so much to me, give me*
> *one more thing—a grateful heart!*
> —GEORGE HERBERT

Chapter 12
JOYFULLY THANKING GOD

The Necklace

JENNA MITCHELL

During the winter of my sophomore year of high school, I counted the days until summer vacation. Regardless of the number of days left, I still dressed for school, tested my blood, took my shot, ate, ran out the door, and headed to my first-period class.

It had been a difficult year for me. Being at a new school is challenging for most kids. It didn't help having to monitor my diabetes and live with other health-related issues. Regardless, I tried to attend class four periods a day and met with a homeschool teacher two days a week. This gave me a full class load.

The highlight of my day was choir class. There I felt accepted. Half of the girls in the choir were typical; the other half was made up of girls with special needs. Though our looks and abilities varied, we all loved lip gloss, new clothes, and singing.

One day our class periods ran short so the entire school could gather at the amphitheater for the Holiday Wish Fairy Assembly. For a moment the only wish I had was that I was back at the Christian high school I had attended my freshman year. How I wished that it didn't have to close!

Since I had never been to a Holiday Wish Fairy Assembly before, I had no idea what to expect. I sat back and waited for it to be over. The assembly began with announcements, and then the wishing part began. One by one members of the Associated Student Body (ASB) cabinet called various students to the stage. Each student made a wish. One wished for a car, another a dog, and the dreaming went on.

This is a dumb assembly! I thought.

Soon all eyes were on Elizabeth, a girl from my choir. What's she doing up there? I wondered. For a girl with special needs—she sure has guts!

Elizabeth stepped in front of the microphone. Without a tremble in her voice, she began to talk. "My wish today is that I could give Jenna Mitchell a present in front of the school."

Jenna Mitchell? That's me! My heart began to pound.

Within seconds, a member of the ASB announced, "Would Jenna Mitchell please come up to meet Elizabeth?"

Without thinking I rose to my feet and began the long walk to the stage. With the entire school watching, I smiled at Elizabeth, then stood by her side.

Elizabeth began her short monologue that she had rehearsed several times. "I want to thank Jenna for being my best friend at school, and I want to give her this necklace."

Extending her hand toward mine, Elizabeth gave me a small gold box tied with a matching ribbon. As the students watched, I thanked Elizabeth and gave her a hug.

With tears in my eyes, I returned to my seat. Suddenly I realized I did have friends at my new school. I also had a best friend—one who understood how it felt to be different, who knew what it was like to have special needs, and who, like me, loved to sing!

∞

Jenna felt nervous when she changed schools. Yet in her new school she found a friend who joyfully sang with her when she was on a mountaintop and walked silently beside her through her valleys. She experienced pure friendship, a friendship that not only shared her tough times but one that celebrated her successes.

Elizabeth understood Jenna's health issues and was thrilled each day Jenna was able to attend class. Jenna, in return, loved Elizabeth and let her know how important she was. These two girls learned early in life that to have a friend they needed to be a friend. They saw beyond each other's disabilities and into each other's hearts. They were able to do this because their parents showed them how.

Our "special" kids thrive when given the tools to do so. Their cups can overflow when taught to see their cup as half full rather than half empty. They are willing to experiment and try new things when they are encouraged to do so. They are willing to love others when loved themselves.

Diane Pitts knew what it was to love a child with special needs. She listened to a child's dreams and then went out of her way to help this dream come true. To this day she can still remember the sounds of Bernadette's "Tapping Toes."

Tapping Toes
DIANE H. PITTS

"Don't get emotionally involved," my college professors advised me, but I'm afraid I didn't listen. Even after twenty-five years of opening my heart to patients in my private practice, I don't regret participating in their walks of pain and joy. Their footprints have altered my life. One set of those footprints belonged to a young lady named Bernadette.

In our attempts to slow down the march of muscular dystrophy, we exercised her. Classical strains, contemporary Christian music, and jazz selections accompanied our physical therapy sessions. Ten-year-old Bernadette loved music, but during one home health visit, she remained unusually quiet.

"What's wrong?" I asked. She glanced despondently toward a picture on the wall—a picture of her gracefully dancing.

"Of all the things I miss, it's dancing," she said wistfully. A few minutes elapsed before she continued. Then her expression changed, and with fire in her eyes, she challenged me. "We can do it! We can find a way."

I knew what she was thinking was impossible, so I gently tried redirecting her, but she grew more excited with the thought. Her hands began moving, her feet lightly tapping a melody only she could hear. My mind raced, thinking of a million excuses, but how could I say no?

"Sure, Bernadette, I'd love to help you. Let's see if we can find a way to dance again."

Two weeks later the moment arrived to try out her dream. I prayed Bernadette could stand in the customized frame my husband had built. I clicked on the tape recorder, and music filled the room.

Her mother and I painstakingly maneuvered Bernadette into a standing position. I was wiping the sweat off my face when I first heard it—the tapping of her feet. With a look of ecstasy, Bernadette slowly responded to the music, dancing as her body allowed. Her mother and I exchanged glances through tears. Bernadette merely laughed. A dream from heaven had floated down to earth.

Six years later the time came for me to change jobs, but I never forgot the time Bernadette and I spent together. She and her family turned tragedy into a step-by-step walk of faith. We eventually dismantled the standing frame but never the hope. Bernadette put one dream in a closet only to pick up another. Her life has challenged me to follow my dreams, not stopping when the path was hard or the goal seemed impossible.

Even now, when I least expect it, a sweet tune invades my thoughts. I hear the faint tapping of toes keeping time to the music. A child can dance—even from a wheelchair.

∞

Karen Kosman thinks ten-year-old Bernadette was motivated by a hope so powerful that it enabled her therapist and mom to share her dream. Together they seized the moment, laying down a foundation of encouragement. Instead of the emptiness of failure, they were bathed in a child's laughter, and they joyfully thanked God for Bernadette's tapping toes. Around God's throne there must have been rejoicing at the success of this little girl whose faith overcame an obstacle some said was impossible.

Susan also joyfully thanked God for her two daughters by marriage and their decision to keep her grandsons, Daniel and Steven, in the family through an "Adoption of Love."

Adoption of Love

SUSAN TITUS OSBORN

"We've made our decision," my daughter-in-law said firmly. "We're going to adopt Daniel."

"You are? I think that's wonderful!" I replied while wrapping my arms around Michele.

"Eric and I talked it over, and we prayed about it. We've decided to do it. By the way, did you hear? Robyn and Clint have decided to adopt Steven too."

Tears came to my eyes, and a sense of relief rushed over my body. I now knew that my young grandsons had found homes within our family. I paused for a moment and thanked God for my two exceptional daughters by marriage.

Trying not to cry, I finally spoke. "I really admire you and Robyn for taking on this added responsibility. The boys will thrive with you parenting them. And this way Rick will be able to see his kids."

I thought back to the day four years before when my stepson, Rick, had married Christina. We were all so happy for him, pleased he had found a young woman with whom to share his life. Although both are mentally challenged, they can function on their own, and he was obviously in love with his new bride.

They rented an apartment, and soon Christina became pregnant. Rick and his wife seemed to handle their own day-to-day needs, but we were concerned that they wouldn't be capable of caring for a newborn. Yet after Steven was born, they surprised us. Christina nursed him, and they worked hard at changing and bathing him. A social services worker checked on them regularly and, at first, was pleased with their efforts.

All went smoothly until Steven started crawling, walking, and getting into things. Then several accidents resulted in trips to the emergency room. Rick and Christina didn't mean for Steven to get hurt; they just didn't have the mental skills to watch him closely or the discernment to prevent such accidents.

Soon Christina was pregnant again, and Daniel was born. Four weeks later Steven ended up in the emergency room with yet another injury. Child Protective Services yanked the boys out of the home and put them in foster care. After months of paperwork and several foster homes, each boy was placed under the foster care of an aunt and uncle—Steven being placed with Robyn and Clint, and Daniel with Michele and Eric. Now, a year later, it was time to decide if this should become a permanent solution.

Daniel's jabbering brought me back to the present. I looked at my daughter-in-law as she held my grandson, pondering the responsibility she was undertaking. With three school-age children of her own, she would have her hands full. I also admired my stepdaughter, Robyn, who was willing to make room in her family of seven for one more to call her Mommy.

I leaned over and hugged Michele again. "Dick and I will support you in this decision 100 percent," I said, choking on my words. I understood the huge responsibility these families were assuming, and I also knew the love that motivated them. Daniel had been subject to seizures and still wasn't talking, but it was too early to determine what handicapping conditions he might possess. Steven seemed typical, but it was too soon to know for sure.

Ready to play, Daniel reached out his arms toward me, and a big smile formed on his face. I hugged my precious little grandson and held him tightly. Silently I thanked God that Daniel would remain in our family for his entire life, and I would always be able to hold him in my arms. Rick eventually accepted the fact that he and Christina couldn't take care of their young sons, and he also thanked God for his brother and sister and their spouses, who had agreed to an adoption of love.

"How lovingly God worked out the arrangement in Susan's family so that little Steven and Daniel ended up with more love, not less—more family, not less," writes Bonnie Hanson. "How tenderly everyone pulled together to consider the needs of these two children, the children they already had, and the two boys' parents as well. God helped change what could have been a tragedy into a blessing for all. This wasn't easy, and it would require great sacrifice, but it was a decision, rich and enduring, that they would never regret.

"These blessings aren't always the ones we've expected. Rick and Christina certainly had not planned for anything to happen to their dearly beloved family. But God was working right there with them, even in the hardest times. And as they followed him, step-by-step in faith, he provided the best and wisest path for them to take."

The parents in the following story, likewise, needed to hold tightly to God's promises as they sought to follow him through some very daunting changes in their plans. They held on to God's promise in 2 Samuel 22:26, 29: "To the faithful you show yourself faithful. . . . You are my lamp, O LORD; the LORD turns my darkness into light" (NIV).

Even when all seemed hopeless, God was there beside them to guide and protect them. He turned their darkest hours into blessings of peace, love, and closeness to him, and he longs to do the same for you. That's how much he loves you and every other parent and caregiver of children with special needs, and how much he loves your children, because they are "Fearfully and Wonderfully Made."

Fearfully and Wonderfully Made
ALI WOLF AS TOLD TO CHARLENE A. DERBY

After my husband and I married, our family grew rapidly. Our first-born, Mark, joined us in January 1986. Twenty-one months later, Jamie and Joey, fraternal twins, joined him to make a terrific trio. Our lives were full. Yet we still hoped to have more children.

Nine years and three miscarriages later, our prayers were answered. I was pregnant! We could hardly contain our excitement as the initial ultrasound revealed twins. Within three weeks a second ultrasound revealed triplets. Then at fourteen weeks, the technician noted that the third sac contained two babies. We were having quads!

As we left the office after the last ultrasound, the doctor handed my husband a card. Rob slid it into his pocket, not showing it to me until we were in the car on the way home. It read: "Dr. Amos, High Risk Specialist, specializing in selective reduction."

I felt a chill run down my spine. For miles we sat speechless. I finally broke the silence and turned toward my husband. "You wouldn't want to do this? Would you?"

"No," he replied with certainty, "I wouldn't."

Several days later my curiosity got the best of me. I wanted to know how the "reduction procedure" was handled. I called the number on the card and explained that I was pregnant with quads. "Two are identical," I told the nurse, "and two are fraternal."

Surprisingly, her manner was brisk and professional but lacking compassion. Sounding as if she were sorting produce in a grocery bin, she reported, "We'll dispose of the identical ones. They present the highest risk. The tissue will be absorbed, and you'll carry the fraternal ones to term."

Immediately a lump formed in my throat. Wanting to hear no more, I ended our conversation and called Rob at work. "Can you believe it?" I cried. "She talked about my babies as if they weren't people!" I continued to rant as Rob tried to calm me down.

"Ali," he said, "why did you even call her? Honey, we would never *reduce* the gift that God has given us."

Three months later our quads were born. At twenty-eight weeks gestation and twelve weeks premature, they were definitely small. Each baby was resuscitated at birth and placed on a ventilator in neonatal intensive care. We weren't allowed to touch or hold them. Prayers of family, friends, and hospital staff carried us through the next year. As I look back on those stress-filled weeks and months, I see four miracles weaving themselves into one tapestry of grace.

Samantha was the only girl. When she was four weeks old (equal to thirty-two weeks gestation time), she experienced retinopathy. Laser surgery was recommended, and as my husband and I waited, the nurses came out to pray with us. After four hours of surgery, my heart sank as the doctor gave us the news, "Samantha may not have vision."

Yet today Samantha is a busy preschooler with glasses. She has normal vision in her left eye but is legally blind in her right eye. She is a dainty girl who loves to sing and dance. When she grows up, she wants to wear makeup and be a mommy. She even says she wants five, six, or seven children! We thank God for the wonderful gift of sight for her.

Adam is our other fraternal quad. He experienced a brain hemorrhage three days after birth, and he has brain damage, hydrocephalus, and cerebral palsy. At one year he underwent surgery to receive a shunt. Today he uses a wheelchair and a walker for mobility. He continues to experience epileptic seizures and some short-term memory issues. Adam is our singer and resident joke teller. He brings joy and laughter into our home. When Adam grows up, he wants to be a firefighter—

from a wheelchair. Yes, our world needs more people who, like Adam, dream big dreams.

Mike is one of our identical twin quads. He weighed only one pound, thirteen ounces at birth. Yet he did the best of the four in the NICU. Today he's a tiny, yet spunky, guy who loves Captain Hook. One might think that Mike is quiet and innocent. Yet we know that he has big plans for some mischievous fun!

Danny is our other identical twin in the quads. He remained on a ventilator for nine weeks and was diagnosed with a congenital heart defect. He fought the odds to live and needed heart surgery. The doctors told us we should attempt to correct the congenital heart defect if we wanted Danny to live but warned us that there was only a 50-percent chance he would survive the surgery since he was so small.

My husband and I authorized the surgery. Together with oldest son, Mark, we followed Danny to the doors of the operating room. The doctor met us and prayed with us. Then I gently kissed my baby's cheek.

Four hours later the doctor joined us in the waiting room. We took one look at his exhausted face and feared the worst. He sat down beside me and put his hand on my knee.

"Well," he said as a smile crossed his face, "do you want the good news or the good news? Danny is doing fine. I didn't tell you this before the surgery, but Danny is the smallest baby on record in the United States to have this operation."

Words could not express our feelings.

Today Danny has a heart murmur, but there are no restrictions on his physical activities. He is our gentle, compassionate child who loves to snuggle. For now Danny wants to learn to play tennis, but his future goal is to become an astronaut!

A few days ago the quads were playing the "running game," which included Adam being carried by Mark. My husband came home to a chaotic house with no hope of peace and quiet until they were tucked in bed asleep. We sat together on the sofa, watching the five of them play. We thought back four years to the day the quads were born and marveled how God had taken perfect care of them.

Yes, our children are truly gifts from God, and we are thankful.

Ali found her life headed down a different path than was planned. Four precious children with special needs were given by God for her to love. Like Ali, Mary the mother of Jesus did not have an easy pregnancy. She felt a certain wonder and awe regarding the child she would conceive. Yet Mary's response to her unplanned pregnancy set the stage for her attitude and acceptance of God's will in her life. "I am the Lord's servant," Mary answered. "May it be to me as you have said" (Luke 1:38 NIV).

Mary's life drastically changed once Jesus entered it. It seems as though Mary left the worrying to her Heavenly Father. She relied on him to speak to Joseph, and she marveled when she heard that he sent an angel to do just that. When she went to visit her close relative, Elizabeth, they were instantly bonded because of the unique gifts God had given them both. Mary must have whispered her words, "May it be to me as you have said," many times.

We trust that when difficult situations arise you might be encouraged by the story of Jesus' birth. Mary also didn't fully understand how God would use her child. She could not see all of God's blessings, and her nine months of pregnancy must have seemed long. Yet Mary obeyed and worshipped God. She quietly accepted her role, trusting completely that God had chosen her for a specific purpose.

Just as God chose Mary to be the mother of Jesus, he has chosen you to love a child with special needs. In his wisdom he has brought this child into your life. You will be forever changed and forever blessed! Linda Evans Shepherd considers the gift of her daughter that God gave her to be "The Best Gift."

The Best Gift

LINDA EVANS SHEPHERD

What's the most important gift a person can give? My daughter gives it often, even though she has to sit in a wheelchair and does not have the ability to speak.

Sometimes I get tired of dealing with people who inquire about her. Usually our conversation starts with the casual question, "Do you have any children?"

I try to avoid saying I have a child who is handicapped because the person asking the question is usually not ready to get emotionally involved with my problems.

But the original "Do you have kids?" question is usually followed by "What school does your daughter go to?"

Unfortunately this probe seems to open the door to conversation chaos.

"Laura goes to two schools," I explain, "one for kids with special needs and one for typical kids."

"Special needs?" I'm asked. "Is your daughter all right?"

Inwardly, I grimace. I've been down this road of explanation before, and I know what is about to happen. "She's a happy little girl," I say, "but she's handicapped."

"What's wrong?"

"She was in a car accident when she was eighteen months old," I explain.

Shock engulfs the person's features. Desperate to make Laura's situation all right, the individual asks, "But she's OK now, right?"

To me, this is a difficult question. Of course I think she's OK. I know she's only handicapped. I also know most people won't understand that. So I say, "Well, Laura's in a wheelchair."

More desperate than ever, the person asks, "But she can talk and stuff, right?"

I sigh. There's no way out of this one. "No, but she can communicate with tongue signals."

By this time my inquirer is at a loss for words. So I try to help out. "But you know, Laura's a happy little girl who really enjoys life."

The person nods mutely and steps back as if ready to make a run for it.

I step closer. "She really is a happy child, and she has lots of friends."

"Oh, she's lucky she has you for a mother."

I force a smile and say, "As far as I'm concerned, I'm just a mother who is lucky to have such a sweet kid for a daughter!"

Then the person excuses herself, and I'm left feeling unsettled. If only I could explain the validity of Laura's life in a way the casual conversationalist could understand. Unfortunately, our society is not taught to recognize the viability of a life that can offer nothing to the world except love.

First Corinthians 13:1–2 says, "If I speak the languages of men and of angels, but do not have love, I am a sounding gong or a clanging cymbal. If I have [the gift of] prophecy, and understand all mysteries and all knowledge, and if I have all faith, so that I can move mountains, but do not have love, I am nothing."

I think the gift of love Laura so freely gives is worth more than any other gift that even an able-bodied person can offer. I have a child who not only receives love but radiates love to all those around her. I am a fortunate mother indeed.

Like Linda, we are fortunate indeed! We are privileged to love and be loved by a child with special needs. We have been forever touched, forever changed, and forever blessed!

Through the last eighteen years, Jenna has richly blessed Janet's life. Janet says, "I'm honored that God choose me to walk through life by Jenna's side. Being Jenna's mother has been one of the highlights of my life! From infancy to maturing into a beautiful young woman and through the challenges of parenting a child with special needs, Jenna has taught me many life lessons. From our experiences together in 'My Treasures, My Friends' to 'The Day My Daughter Lost All Hope' to 'She's Eighteen,' God has been our Master Teacher. Yet no lesson has been as valuable as the lesson I learned the day she was born—and I joyfully and enthusiastically thank God for 'The Gift of Love, the Gift of Life.'"

The Gift of Love, the Gift of Life
JANET LYNN MITCHELL

I stood in awe as her contractions progressed. Gently I dried her forehead from the sweat of labor. One moment we laughed, and the next I wiped her countless tears. We both knew that today our lives would change forever.

Within hours her contractions intensified. The doctor finally arrived. Quickly we moved to the delivery room. The coldness of the room was warmed by the miracle about to take place. I sat by her side, brushing her hair away from her face as I continued to coach her. With one final push, the baby emerged. The doctor cut the cord, separating mother and child.

The room was silent, except for the first sounds of a healthy cry. For a moment time seemed to stand still. I took a deep breath as the nurse carefully bundled the precious newborn and then laid her in my arms—my arms. The young woman who had just given birth had chosen me to become the mother of her child.

As I touched and cradled Jenna for the first time, I glanced at her biological mother out of the corner of my eye. As our eyes met, they spoke volumes. I nodded to assure her of my sanctioned vows to motherhood. I held my newborn daughter and brought her to the lips of her biological mother. Taking a mental picture, I watched the final kiss good-bye.

My voice quivered as I tried to find appropriate words to express my thanks. She smiled at me as tears streamed down her face. I saw her struggle as I began to bond with my priceless, special gift.

Walking to the newborn nursery, I gasped at my own thoughts. The image of God the Father played in slow motion across my mind. I tried to imagine how God had reacted the moment his Son, Jesus, was born. I pictured God beholding his infant Son. I imagined him touching his Holy Child and cradling him within his bosom. Perhaps tears had formed in God's eyes as he conceived the provision, the plan he had created for the redemption of my sins. I wondered if God, too, lifted baby Jesus to his lips, kissing his Son good-bye as he handed Mary his Son. I cried as I could not find words to express my thanks.

Before this day I had never comprehended such an act of love. It was courageous, unselfish love that motivated the gift of life my daughter received. It was joy unspeakable to be given a child, to become a family. The memories of this day will forever be treasured. For through this experience I, for the first time, began to understand how deeply God loved me. It became crystal clear to me the price God paid when he gave up his Child—for me.

As I did many years ago, please come and join me in walking to the newborn nursery. See the miracle of God's love—the birth of baby Jesus. Experience the awesome reality that God has chosen you to receive his Child. Look in his eyes, open your heart, and graciously accept as God lays his Son into your arms.

May you receive the gift of love that God so fully gives, the gift of joy, the gift of the Christ Child.

Conclusion

God gives *A Special Kind of Love* to those in whose care he entrusts children with special needs. This love walks in faith, conquers fear, and accepts the unacceptable. The miracle of this love is that it never ends.

Throughout this book you have seen this love in action. Parents, grandparents, foster parents, and extended families as well as teachers, doctors, social workers, friends of the family, and pastors have shared how loving one child has touched their lives. One parent said it this way: "I have loved, and I'll never be the same."

The journey of caring for a child with special needs is not meant to be traveled alone. Families, friends, and churches often provide support in helping to meet the child's needs. There are, however, times when additional information and support are needed; therefore, we have provided the following resources to aid you.

May your journey be blessed as you experience *A Special Kind of Love*.

RESOURCES

TASK (Team of Advocates for
 Special Kids)
100 W. Cerritos Ave.
Anaheim, CA 92805
www.TASKca.org
taksca@yahoo.com

Christian Council on Persons with
 Disabilities
1100 W. 42nd Street, Suite 223
Indianapolis, IN 46208
Phone: (317) 923-CCPD [2273]
info@ccpd.org
www.ccpd.org

JAF Ministries (Joni and Friends)
PO Box 3333
Agoura Hills, CA 91376
Phone: (818) 707-5664
www.joniandfriends.org

Juvenile Diabetes Research
 Foundation International
120 Wall Street
New York, NY 10005-4001
Phone: (800) 533-CURE [2873]
Fax: (212) 785-9595
info@jdrf.org

NICHCY (National Information
 Center for Children and Youth
 with Disabilities)
PO Box 1492
Washington, DC 20013
Phone: (800) 659-0285
www.nichcy.org

The Arc (formerly the Association
 for the Retarded Citizens of the
 United States)
1010 Wayne Avenue, Suite 650
Silver Spring, MD 20910
Phone: (310) 565-3842
info@the arc.org
www.thearc.org

United Cerebral Palsy Association,
 Inc.
1660 L Street NW, Suite 700
Washington, DC 20036
Phone: (800) 872-5827
ucpnatl@ucp.org
www.ucpnatl@ucp.org

American Psychiatric Association
1000 Wilson Boulevard, Suite 1825
Arlington, VA 22209-3901
Phone: (703) 907-7300
www.psych.org

American Association on Mental
    Retardation
444 N. Capitol Street NW, Suite 846
Washington, DC 20001-1512
Phone: (800) 424-3688
www.aamr.org

American Juvenile Arthritis
    Organization
1300 W. Peachtree Street
Atlanta, GA 30309
Phone:(800) 283-7800
www.arthritis.org

Asthma and Allergy Foundation of
    America
1233 20th Street NW, Suite 402
Washington, DC 20036
Phone: (800) 7-ASTHMA
    [727-8462]
info@aafa.org
www.aafa.org

National Attention Deficit Disorder
1788 Second Street, Suite 200
Highland Park, IL 60035
Phone: (847) 432-ADDA [2332]
mail@add.org
www.add.org

National Autism Hotline/Autism
    Services
605 Ninth Street, Prichard Building
PO Box 507
Huntington, WV 25710-0507
Phone: (304) 525-8014

Birth Defect Research for Children,
    Inc.
930 Woodcock Road, Suite 225
Orlando, FL 32803
www.birthdefects.org

Association for Children with Down
    Syndrome
4 Fern Place
Plainview, NY 11779
Phone: (516) 933-4700
info@acds.org
www.acds.org

Epilepsy Foundation
4351 Garden City Drive
Landover, MD 20785-7223
Phone: (800) EFA-1000 [332-1000]
www.efa.org

National Head Injury Foundation
1776 Massachusetts Avenue NW,
    Suite 100
Washington, DC 20036-1904
Phone: (202) 296-6443

Alexander Graham Bell Association
    for the Deaf
2000 M Street NW, Suite 310
Washington, DC 20036
Phone: (202) 337-5220
www.agbell.org

American Heart Association
    National Center
7272 Greenville Avenue
Dallas, TX 75231-4596
Phone: (800) 242-8721
www.americanheart.org

Learning Disabilities Association of
    America
4156 Library Road
Pittsburgh, PA 15234
Phone: (412) 341-1515

National Center for Learning
    Disabilities
381 Park Avenue S., Suite 1401
New York, NY 10016
Phone: (212) 545-7510
www.ld.org

Muscular Dystrophy Association
3300 E. Sunrise Drive
Tucson, AZ 85718-3208
Phone: (800) 572-1717
mda@mdausa.org
www.mdausa.org

Spina Bifida Association of America
4590 MacArthur Boulevard NW, NY
    Suite 250
Washington, DC 20007-4226
Phone: (800) 621-3141
sbaa@sbaa.org
www.sbaa.org

The Elizabeth M. Boggs Center in
    Developmental Disabilities
Robert Wood Johnson Medical
    School
335 George Street
PO Box 2688
New Brunswick, NJ 08903-2688
Phone: (732) 235-9300

FOCUS ON THE FAMILY®

Welcome to the Family!

Whether you received this book as a gift, borrowed it,
or purchased it yourself, we're glad you read it. It's just one of
the many helpful, insightful, and encouraging resources
produced by Focus on the Family.

In fact, that's what Focus on the Family is all about—
providing inspiration, information, and biblically based
advice to people in all stages of life.

It began in 1977 with the vision of one man, Dr. James Dobson,
a licensed psychologist and author of 18 best-selling books on
marriage, parenting, and family. Alarmed by the societal, political,
and economic pressures that were threatening the existence of
the American family, Dr. Dobson founded Focus on the Family
with one employee and a once-a-week radio broadcast aired
on only 36 stations.

Now an international organization, the ministry is dedicated to
preserving Judeo-Christian values and strengthening and encouraging families through the life-changing message of Jesus Christ.
Focus ministries reach families worldwide through 10 separate
radio broadcasts, two television news features, 13 publications,
18 Web sites, and a steady series of books and award-winning
films and videos for people of all ages and interests.

• • • •

For more information about the ministry, or if we can be of help to your
family, simply write to Focus on the Family, Colorado Springs, CO
80995 or call (800) A-FAMILY (232-6459). Friends in Canada may
write Focus on the Family, PO Box 9800, Stn Terminal, Vancouver, BC
V6B 4G3 or call (800) 661-9800. Visit our Web site—www.family.org—
to learn more about Focus on the Family or to find out if there is an
associate office in your country.

We'd love to hear from you!